WIDNES

THROUGH TIME

Jean & John Bradburn

AMBERLEY PUBLISHING

First published 2012

Amberley Publishing
The Hill, Stroud, Gloucestershire, GL5 4EP
www.amberley-books.com

Copyright © Jean & John Bradburn, 2012

The right of Jean & John Bradburn to be identified as the
Author of this work has been asserted in accordance with
the Copyrights, Designs and Patents Act 1988.

ISBN 978 1 4456 0999 7 (print)

British Library Cataloguing in Publication Data.
A catalogue record for this book is available from the
British Library.

Typesetting by Amberley Publishing.
Printed in Great Britain.

Introduction

Widnesians are justly proud of the town's rich history and of their ancestors, who came to the town to work in the harsh surroundings of the soap and chemical works.

The first real settlements of Widnes were established in Upton, Appleton, Farnworth and Ditton. There was an early church at Farnworth. The name is Anglo-Saxon, meaning 'fern'. The Saxon cross still remains at the front of Farnworth church. The ancient township was dominated by the Bold family, who were landowners, from as early as 1042. They were the co-founders of the early chapel at Farnworth which was a chapel of ease to Prescot. The Bold chapel still holds many treasures from Bold Hall, demonstrating the influence of this ancient family on the history of Farnworth and Widnes.

The River Mersey played an important part in the history of Widnes. It is suggested that the name derives from the Danish description of the estuary – wide nose. The first ferry was established by the 6th Baron John Fitz Richard around 1178. James Brindley produced the first plans for a bridge in 1768. Thomas Telford submitted a design in 1814, but in fact the first bridge built was the railway bridge.

The town did not alter much until the huge industrial development that transformed Widnes from the 1830s. Industry grew fast and immigrant workers flowed into the town. Because of the town's strategic position on the Mersey, the chemical industry flourished, resulting in the canals and the rapidly developing railway system. In 1833, the St Helens and Runcorn Gap Railway was opened and the Sankey Canal was extended to Widnes. The Widnes dock was completed the same year and started to handle coal traffic from the railway.

John Hutchinson had established his No. 1 works on Spike Island by 1849. In 1850 William Gossage established his works in West Bank. As industry flourished, the demand for housing for workers led to a housing boom in 1866. The workers also needed their spiritual needs to be provided for; St Mary's was built in 1858 and St Patrick Roman Catholic church in 1888.

The men who came to Widnes to start industry, and who became rich, built fine houses in Appleton, Farnworth, and Hough Green, well away from the chemical fumes of the West Bank.

We cannot forget the importance to the town of rugby league. As early as 1878 we had a Widnes Rugby Football Club. Widnes played a part in the breakaway Northern League and rugby has always held an important place in the heart of the town.

The story of Widnes has influenced the character of the town and its people.

Acknowledgements

Our grateful thanks go Bob Martindale for permission to use his photographs and his vast knowledge of the history of Widnes. To Jean Morris, whose two books *Into the Crucible* and *Where Spring Never Came* are heartfelt and comprehensive histories of the town. She also offered me advice and encouragement. Thanks go to Paul Meara at the Catalyst Museum for his assistance. We must also acknowledge the two-volume work *The Last of England*, a thorough history of the pubs of Widnes by Colin Lawless.

Thank you to Halton Borough Council for permission to use photographs from their collections. Finally, Rosie Parker, from Widnes Library, for her support, enthusiasm and love of her town.

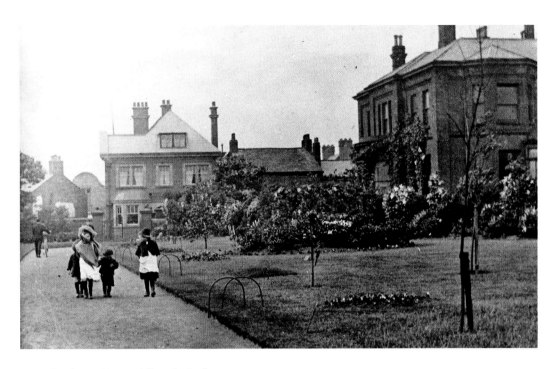

Appleton House, Victoria Park

The house stood where the rose garden is planted in Victoria Park. It was built as the home of Sir Henry Wade Deacon, a local industrialist. We can see the Appleton Arms Hotel, later named the Angel and Elephant. It is now being lovingly redeveloped as a children's nursery. The view now shows mature trees and the flowerbeds celebrating our Queen's Diamond Jubilee.

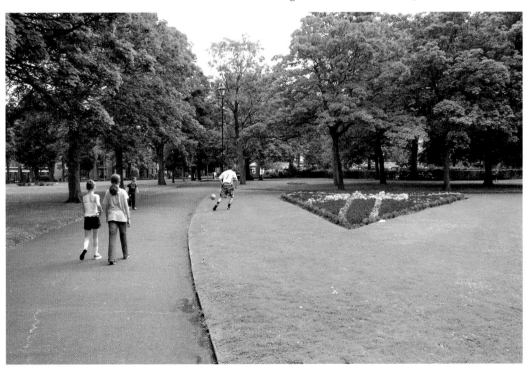

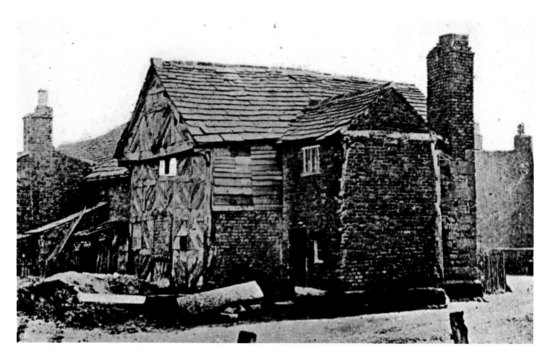

Appleton Hall

Appleton Hall was built for the Appleton family in the sixteenth century and was the home of the Hawarden family. The name Appleton is thought to be derived from the many apple orchards around the village. The hall is long gone but it stood at the top of Appleton village on the site of the old park insulation works.

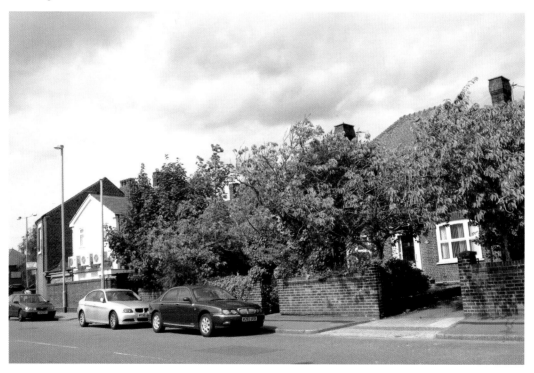

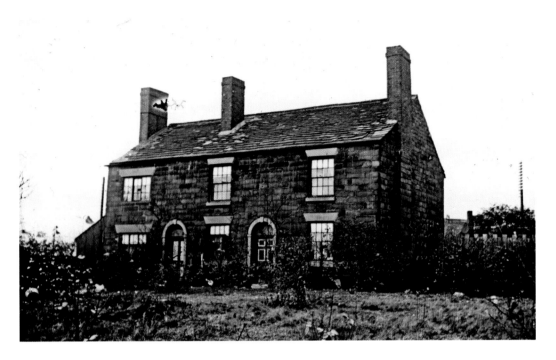

Appleton Lower House

Now this corner of Lower House Lane is dominated by the Albion, but it is the site of a farmhouse built in the reign of Charles I. The 1842 tithe shows the owner to be John Shaw Leigh and the tenant was Elizabeth Houghton. It was used by Catholics as a meeting place; eventually St Bede's Roman Catholic church was built in 1846.

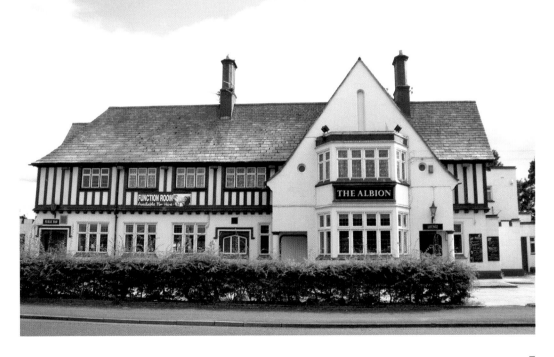

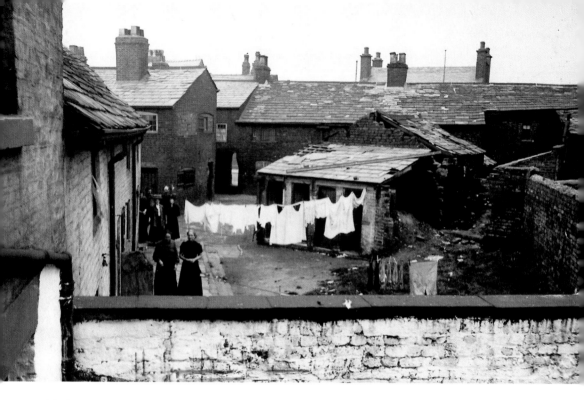

Tithebarn Street

The area was demolished in 1958 but this is a good reminder of the poverty of the time; an example of the old-style courts which were overcrowded and insanitary. This picture shows some distinguished ladies visiting the street and no doubt offering advice to very proud people. Note the washing lines!

Tithes were one tenth of all produce payable to the Church and the area was named for the large barns needed to hold the produce. The area is now dominated by St Bede's and the primary school. It looks like a barn is in the playground.

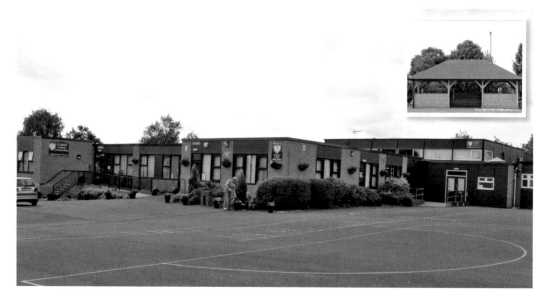

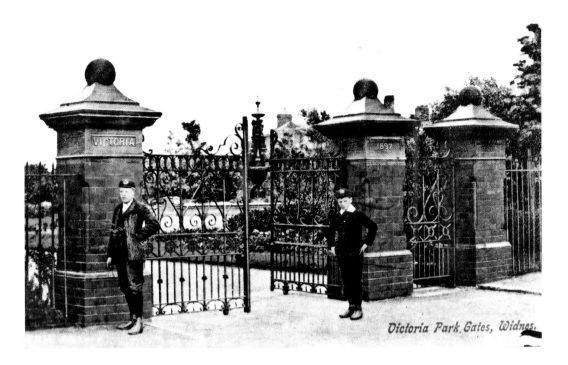

Victoria Park Gates

We love this picture of the park gates. It shows two young men, elegantly dressed, by the fine wrought-iron gates in 1897. The new picture shows the Gladstone fountain and the war memorial in the background. The plaques name the 818 men lost in the First World War and the 289 lost in the Second World War.

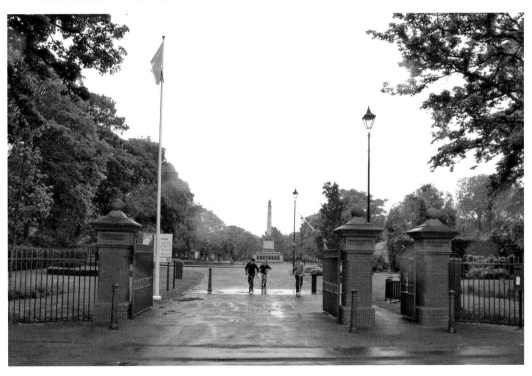

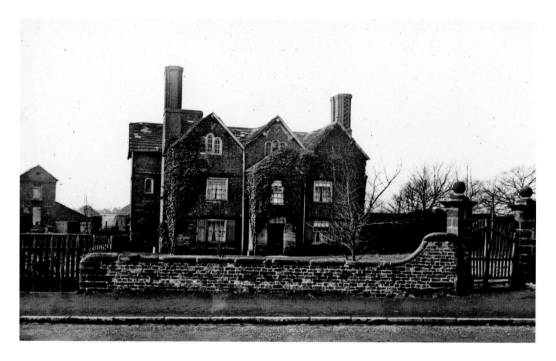

Appleton Upper House

Now we see the very green Widnes Golf Club, but here was the Upper House, sometimes known as Widnes House. The 1842 tithe shows James Cowley as the owner of the house and estate. The building was demolished around 1910 and only the old brewery is still standing. It is now used as a changing room for the golfers.

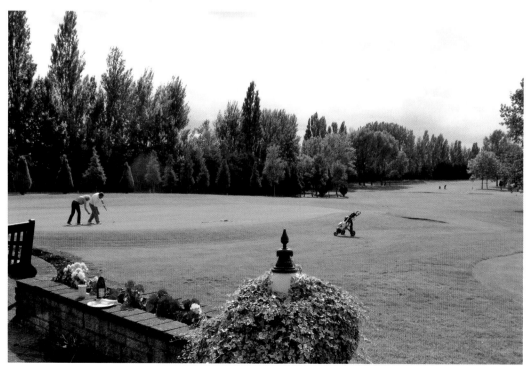

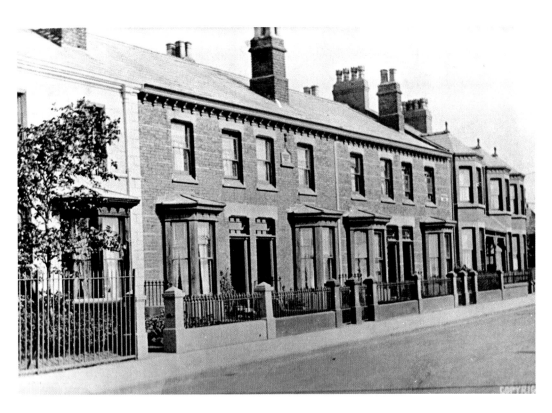

Pineapple Terrace, Birchfield Road

The Appleton's family crest was three pineapples; the crest can still be seen around the corner in Pineapple Terrace on Birchfield Road. The choice of crest is surprising. Why not apples? Perhaps the new exotic fruit was more appealing to the family?

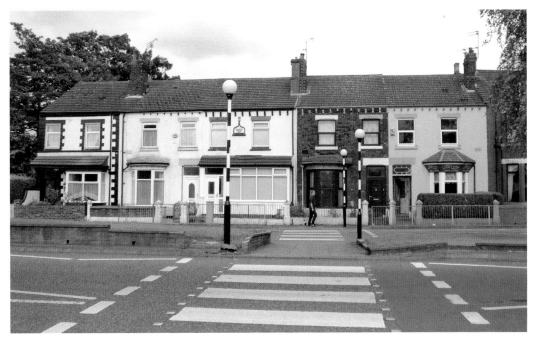

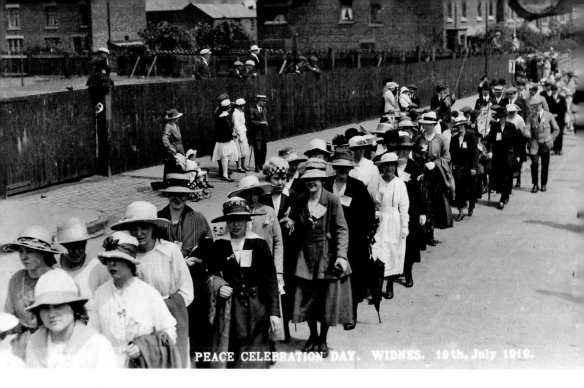

PEACE CELEBRATION DAY. WIDNES. 19th, July 1919.

Peace March, Deacon Road

In 1919 Widnes celebrated the end of the war. The town, like many others, had lost a generation of men and peace was greeted with huge relief. This shows the Peace March, with the people of the town and their children in their Sunday best in Deacon Road. The photographer must have stood on the corner of Frederick Street.

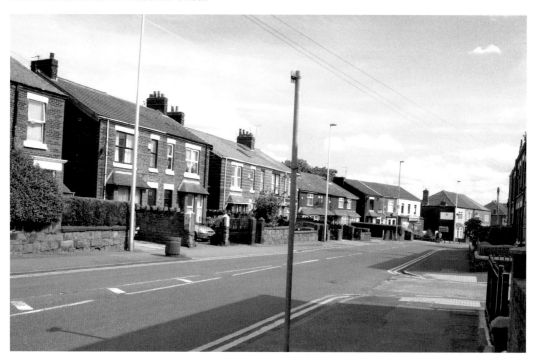

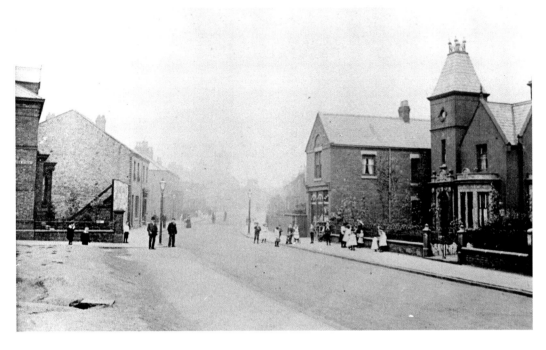

Albert Road from Deacon Road

Albert Road is now a busy, pedestrianised shopping street, but much of this area was cleared to make way for the new market and shopping centre. This is a view towards Peelhouse Lane.

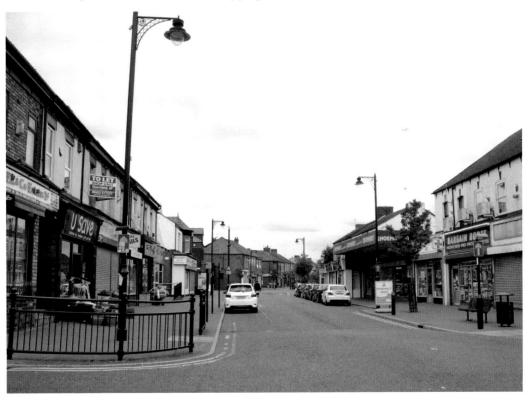

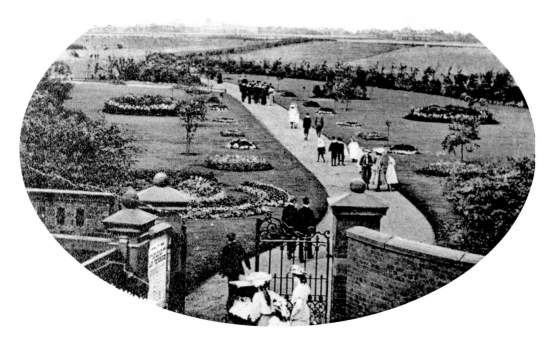

Strolling Victoria Park

Victoria Park opened in 1900 as a memorial to Queen Victoria's Diamond Jubilee celebration. The picture shows elegant figures strolling in the park. The park has now been lovingly restored, with a new bandstand and excellent sporting facilities. The modern view shows how the trees have matured.

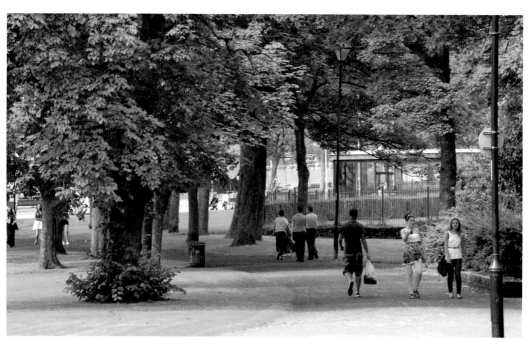

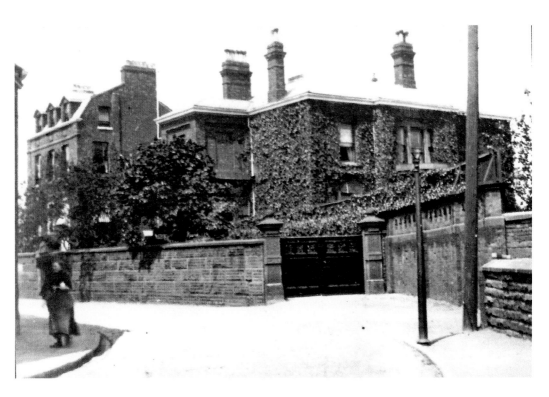

Appleton House
Again we see Appleton House, home of Sir Henry Wade Deacon, taken from Appleton village. The house was demolished in the late 1930s. The estate of Henry Wade Deacon was taken over by Widnes Council in 1876 and was landscaped to be enjoyed by all as a public park in 1900.

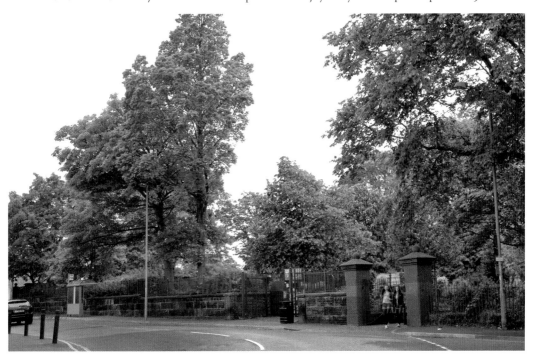

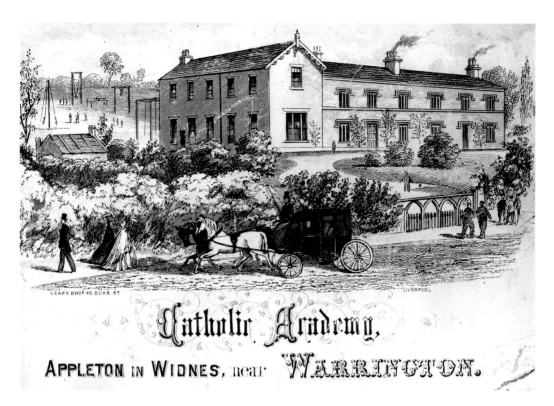

Catholic Academy, APPLETON in WIDNES, near WARRINGTON.

Catholic Academy

Built in 1830 as the Catholic Academy in Highfield Road, it was a boarding school and students came from all over the world; Appleton was a stronghold of Catholicism at the time. This fine terrace has survived and is now known as Appleton Villas.

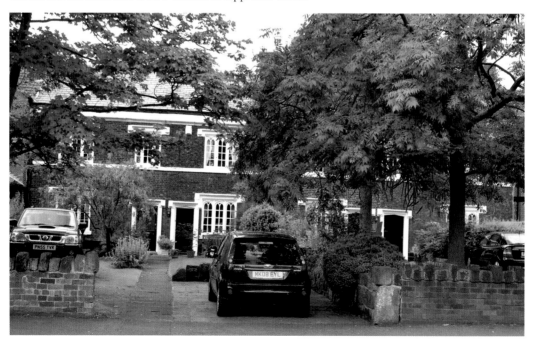

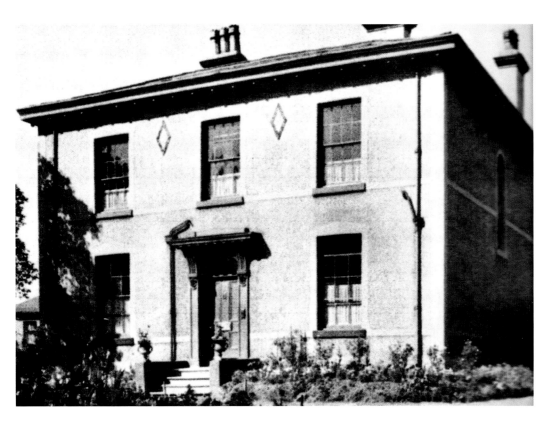

Highfield House

Highfield House was built by John McCellan, a local industrialist who came to Widnes in 1846. He founded the North British Chemical Co., which manufactured borax and alkali. This fine house became a maternity hospital and holds many happy memories. It is still an NHS clinic today.

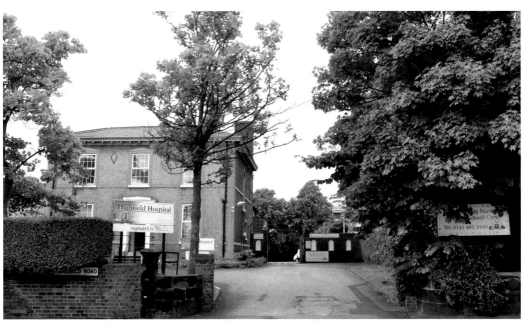

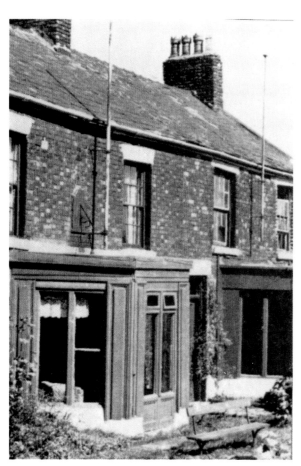

Appleton Lodge

John Hutchinson opened his first factory in 1847. He built this house for his wife and five children in Appleton village, a green and peaceful place to bring up his family, far removed from the smoke and dust of Spike Island. The house was demolished in 1960. It was in Appleton village, near to the car park and old graveyard, which we see in the picture below.

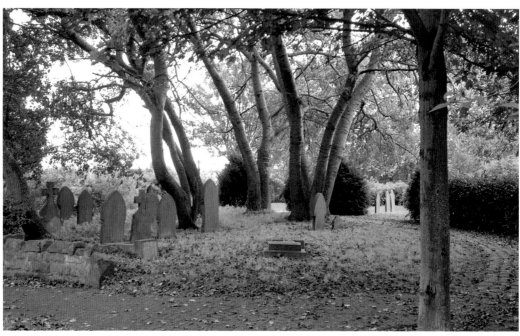

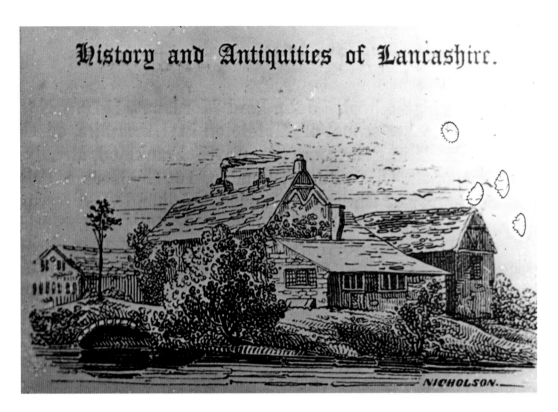

History and Antiquities of Lancashire.

NICHOLSON.

Peel House

The home of William Smyth, who became Bishop of London and founded Farnworth Grammar School. He was also a co-founder of Brasenose College, Oxford. A wealthy man, he also founded a chapel at Farnworth church. Demolished in 1905, it was situated by the attractive green space by Lilac Avenue.

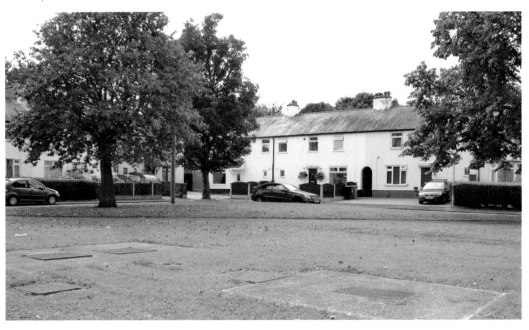

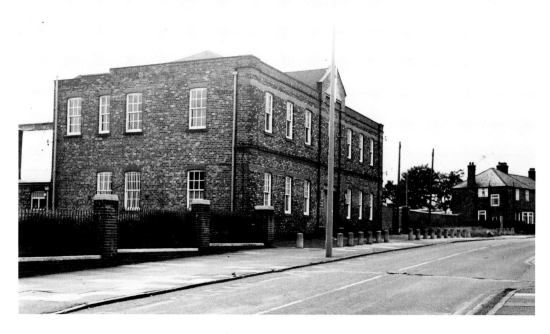

The Barracks, Peel House Lane

The barracks are now a Territorial Army centre, housing the 4th Battalion, Mercian Regiment. Peel House Lane was a country lane until 1910. Beyond the barracks we can see the Peel House Lane estate, built around 1920.

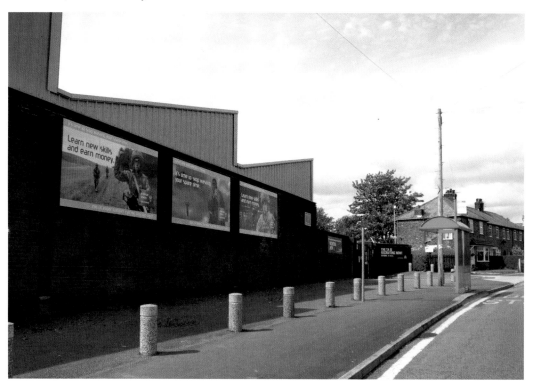

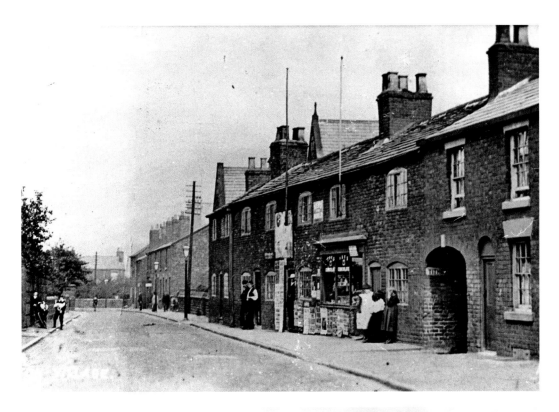

Tithebarn Street

A view of the entrance to Tithebarn Street from Appleton village. This was just past St Bede's church. The 1842 tithe shows the large numbers living in each dwelling. Now St Bede's church is the main feature of the area. The church was built from sandstone from Appleton quarry.

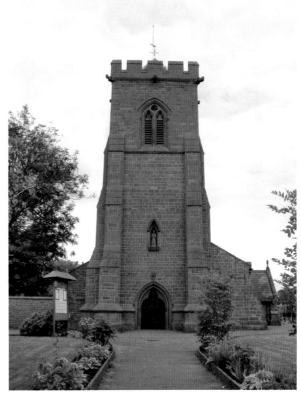

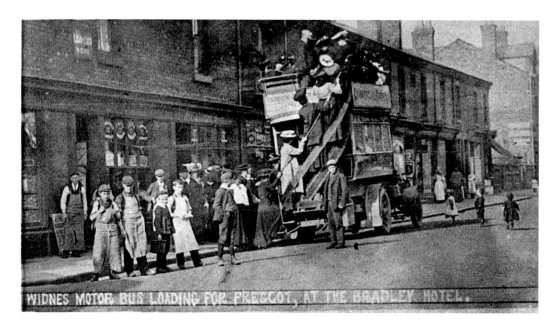

WIDNES MOTOR BUS LOADING FOR PRESCOT, AT THE BRADLEY HOTEL.

Trolley Bus Outside Bradley Hotel, Albert Road

The bus leaving for Prescot around 1908. This was the main bus route in the town. The Bradley Hotel still stands proudly at the corner of this busy street filled with shoppers. The buses still run up Albert Road, although it is closed to other traffic.

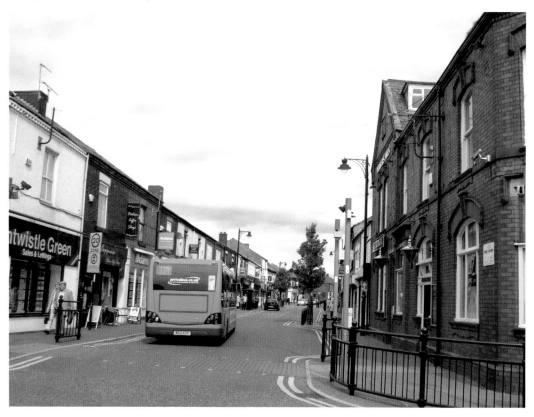

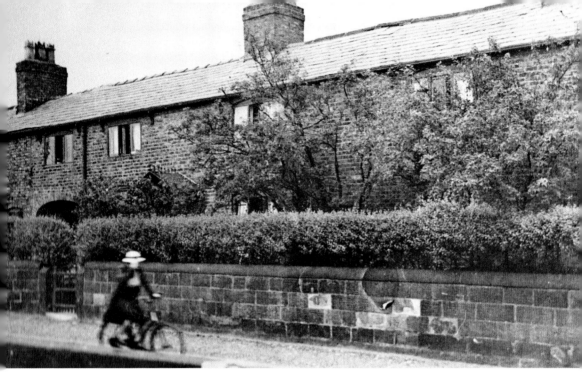

Appleton Terrace

A row of cottages opposite St Bede's church. These cottages had their own cottage industry, which was wire drawing. It was the home of the Hayes family. After demolition it was occupied by the Park Insulation Works and has since been redeveloped as new modern apartments.

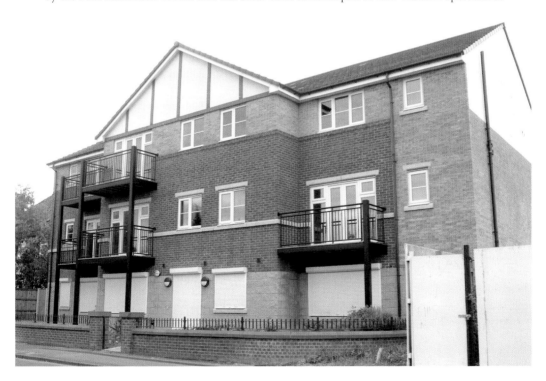

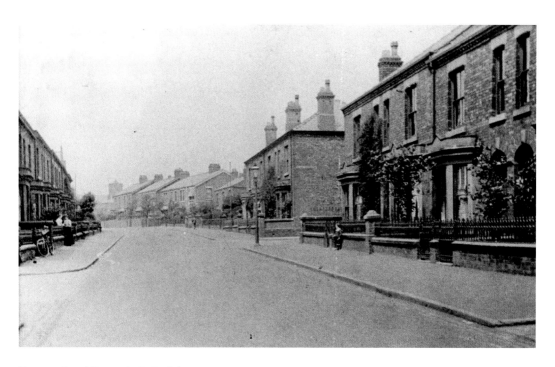

Deacon Road Towards St Bede's
Deacon Road in 1910, looking towards St Bede's church. The terraces were built in the early 1900s. The road was named after Sir Henry Wade Deacon and was the main thoroughfare at the time. This photograph reflects the quiet dignity of the town at this time.

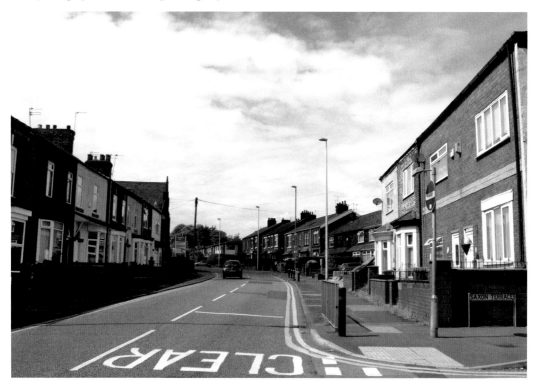

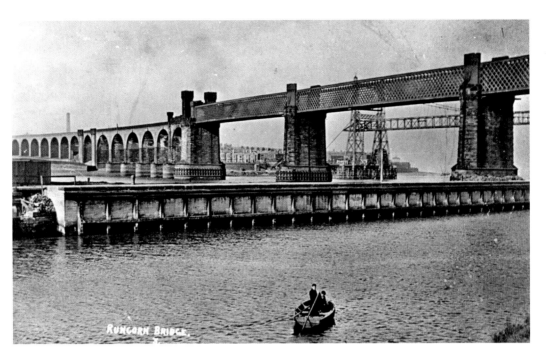

Railway Bridge
Showing the Manchester
Ship Canal, which was
constructed in 1890. The
Transporter can be seen
beyond. The modern
shot was taken from the
Independent Living Centre
in Collier Street.

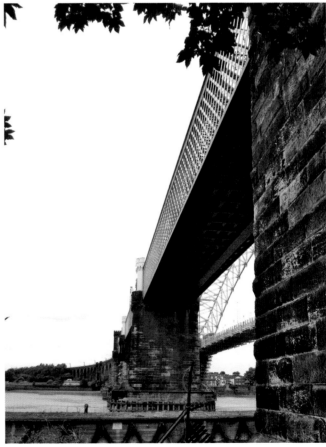

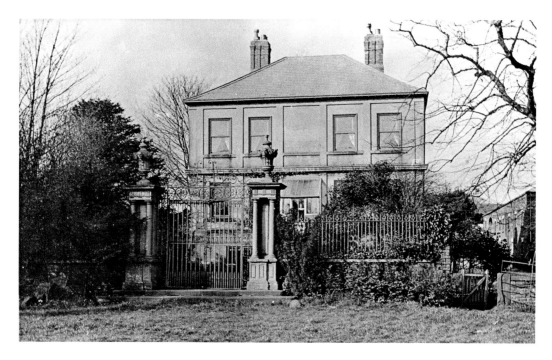

Cronton Hall

Cronton is an old Anglo-Saxon name meaning 'crow town'. The hall was remodelled in 1740, with stables and a coach-house added. The Wright family lived here for over a century, leaving in 1821 when Bartholomew Bretherton bought the hall. The hall was plastered in grey, as it still is today, and the magnificent gates were added. There is sad local story that the gates were always closed after a child ran out and was killed by a passing carriage.

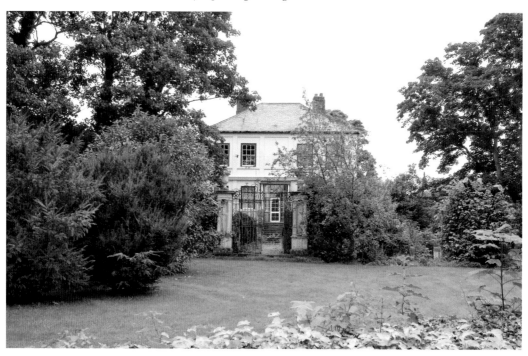

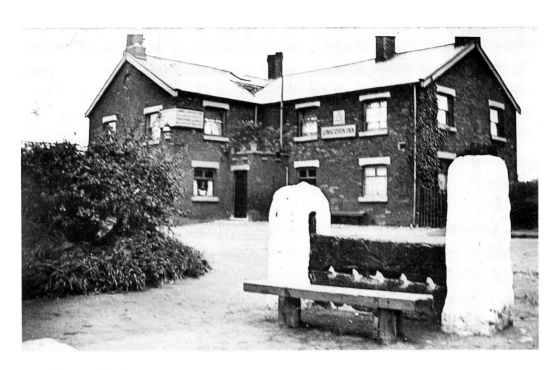

Cronton Stocks

The village stocks were used for punishment of petty offenders. They were confined by their wrists and ankles and are named because of the stakes at each side. Cronton stocks are unusual as they have five holes. They stood by the Unicorn Inn, but were moved in 1955 by Whiston Council and restored by Knowsley Council in 2007.

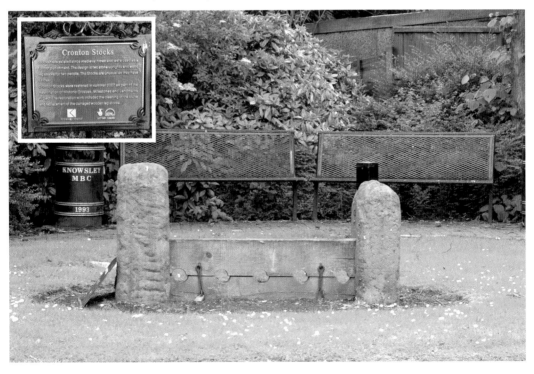

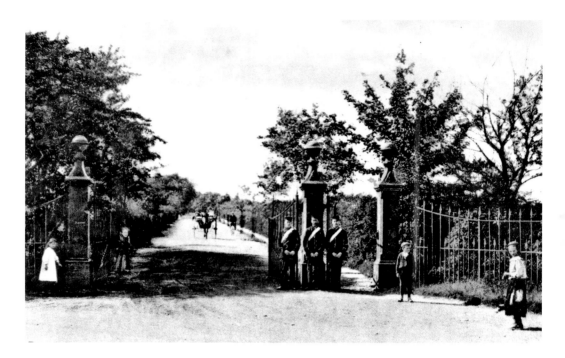

Pexhill Gates

Pexhill is a local beauty spot in Cronton. This early photograph shows the elegance of the time. Visitors have enjoyed the countryside and extensive views for many years. It is now visited by dog walkers, ramblers and climbers exercising their skills in the quarry. Pexhill is an important nature site containing extensive lowland heath.

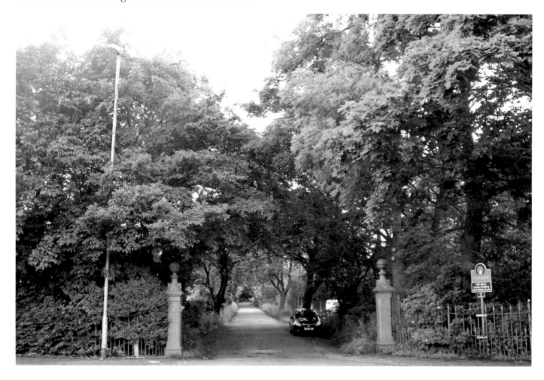

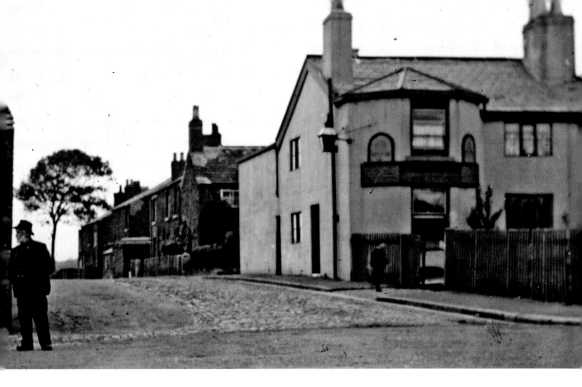

The Beehive Inn

The inn opened around 1848. In 1901 the licence was held by John Pilkington. In 1930, it was sold by Greenall Whitley on the condition that it would never hold a beer licence again. It has now been lovingly renovated as a private home. The building has also been a chip shop, newsagents, and even an antique shop.

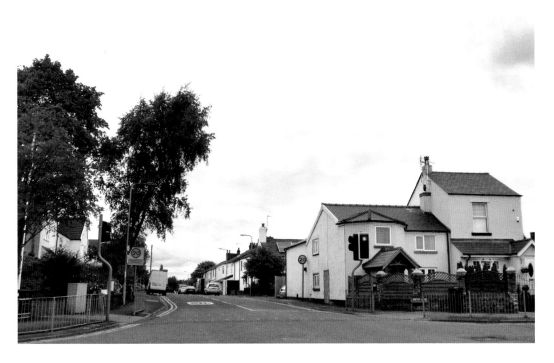

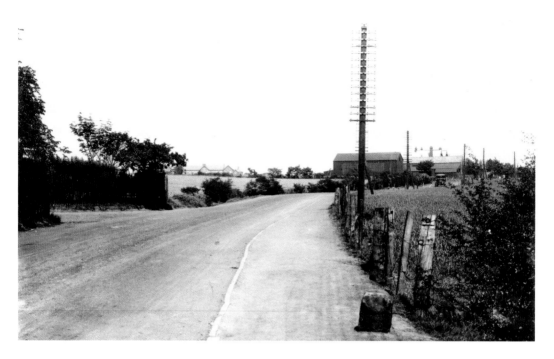

Cronton Lane

This is now a very busy road. The Hill Crest Hotel was built on the site of the original house, so named because the family were named Hill and were local plumbers. It was later used as a school before being demolished in the late 1980s. It is now a thriving hotel.

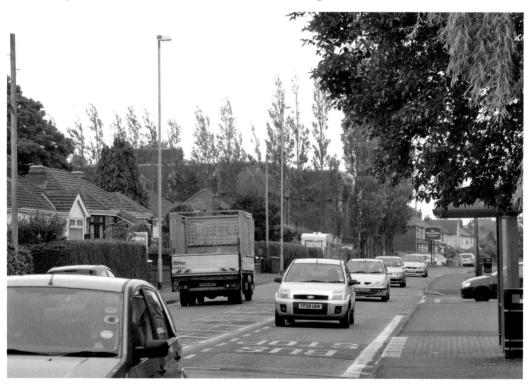

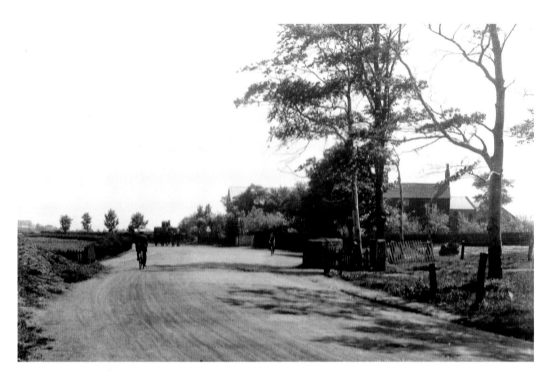

Norlands Lane

A rural view of Norlands Lane in 1922. The 1893 map shows Hanging Birch Farm, Birchfield Cottage, and Norlands House. By 1927, we can see the Farnworth Nautical School (Saint Aidan's), which was built in 1907. This was a reform school for boys; it stood near to where St Aidan's Drive is today.

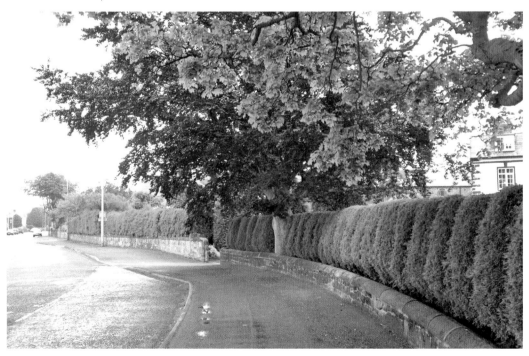

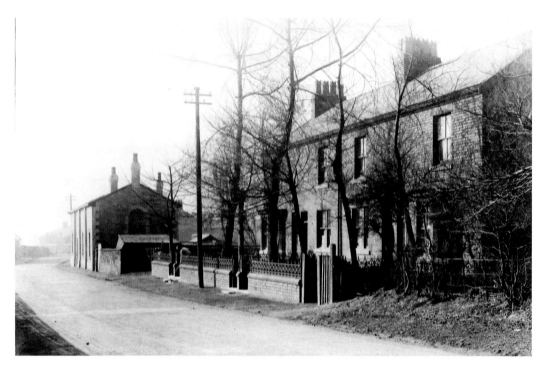

Hale Road Towards St Mary's School

This view down Hale Road shows St Mary's School, built in the 1860s and sometimes known as Ditton Hall School. It was founded by Sarah, daughter of Bartholomew Bretherton. In 1884, a new school was opened in St Michael's Road. The site is now Booth's Garage.

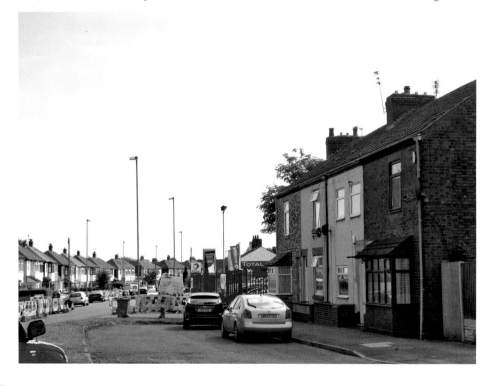

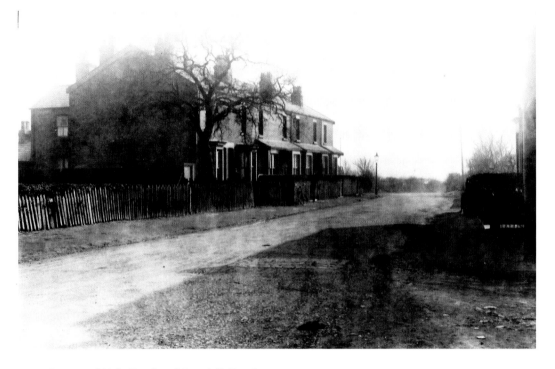

Corner of Hale Road and Dundalk Road

A view in 1922 of the corner of Hale Road. Only one house remains. The rest were demolished in an air raid in 1941. The row suffered a direct hit and a mother, father and two children were killed. A police station was built on the site and although it is not used today, the building remains.

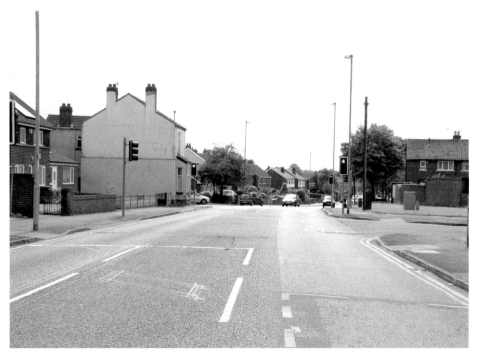

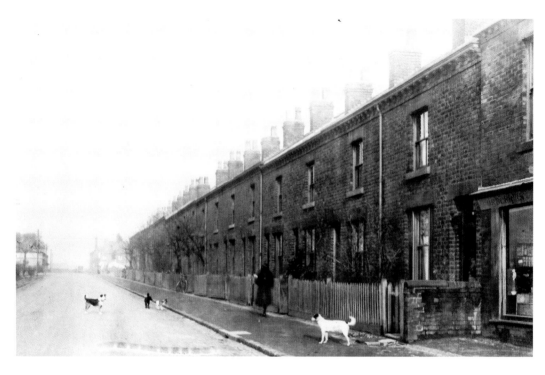

Hale Road Towards Ball O' Ditton

The terrace still stands today, although the general store on the corner has been converted into a house. The houses have lost their front gardens due to road widening. The 1924 Kelly's Directory shows Hale Road to be a busy shopping street, including a boot-repairer and butcher.

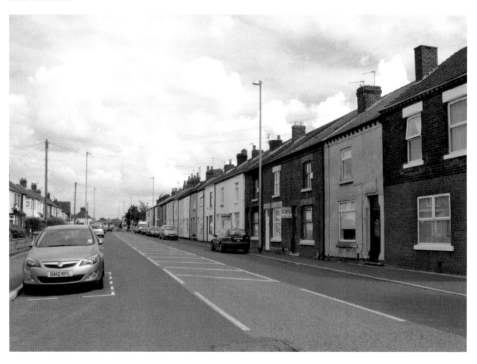

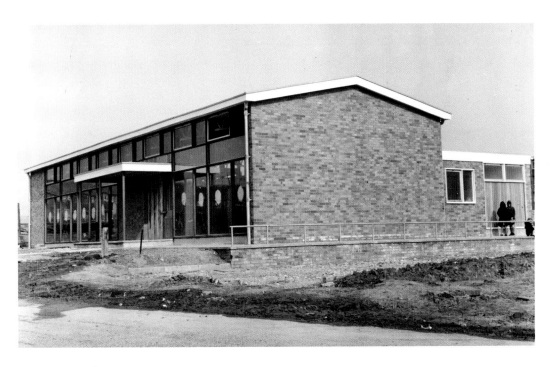

Ditton Library

Ditton Library opened in April 1962. That week, Elvis was top of the charts with 'Wooden Heart' and the Russian cosmonaut Yuri Gagarin became the first man in space. In 2012 the library is celebrating its fiftieth birthday. It has recently been remodelled and is a now also a children's centre and information point for Halton Borough Council.

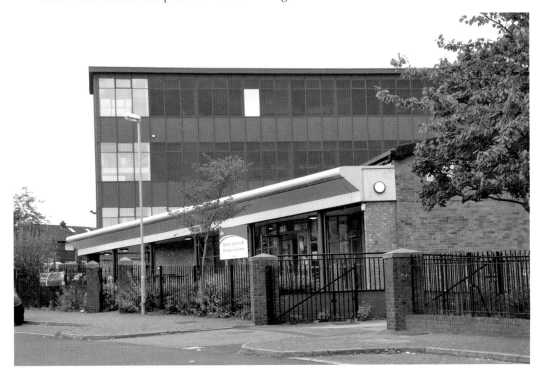

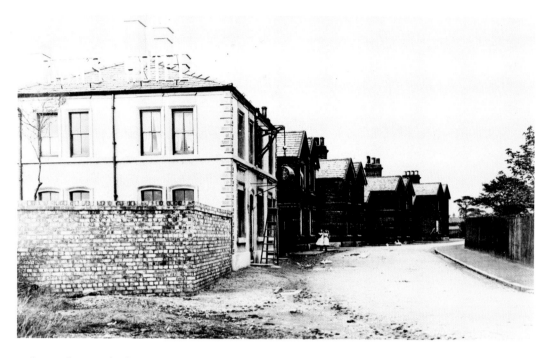

Hale Road Towards the New Inn

Originally called the Ditton Vaults, John Barber was the first landlord. In the 1890s it was bought by Robert Cain & Sons, the Liverpool brewer, and became known as Cain's Hotel. Note the elegant sign on the roof.

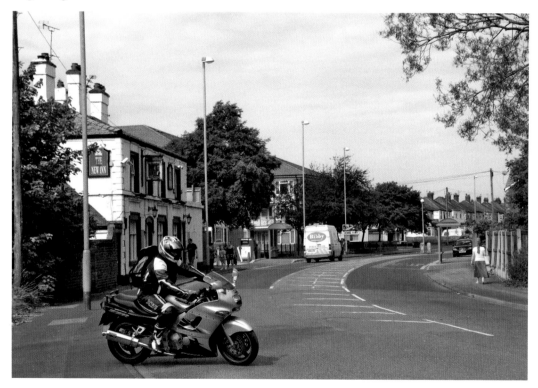

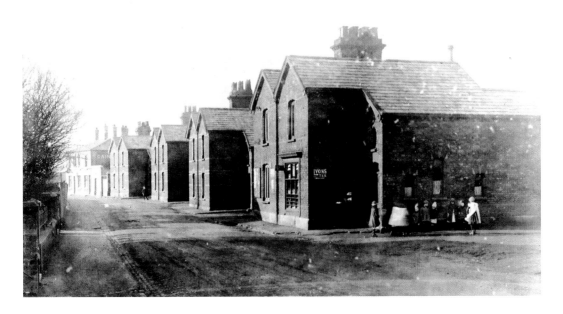

Hale Road

Here we can see Pitville cottages looking down towards the New Inn. The cottages are long gone and we have modern houses and flats. This must have been a busy road leading to Ditton Junction station. Nearby was the Ditton rail disaster of 1912. The holiday express from North Wales derailed, with fifteen people killed and many injured.

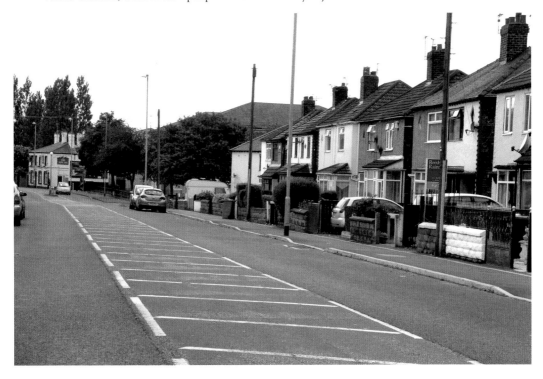

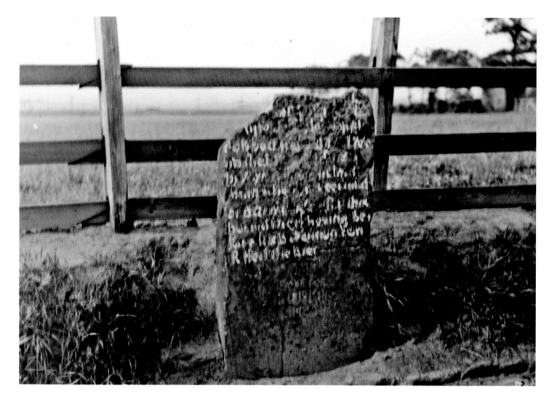

Ditton Murder Stone

This tells the story of the infamous murder of Edward Culshaw at Ditton Bank Farm in 1784. He walked to Liverpool each week to collect £10, this being the farmworkers' wages, from the bank. He was nearly home when he was robbed and murdered. John Thomas was the murderer. He ran from the scene but left a playbill which incriminated him. He was hanged at Lancaster Gaol, having admitted his guilt. The stone now stands in St Michael's church garden in Hough Green.

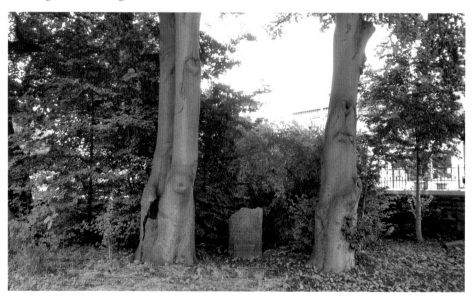

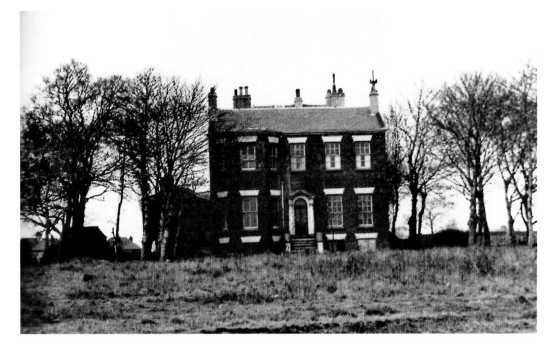

Ditton Lodge

The house is shown on the census as early as 1841. It was occupied by Mary Rothwell, then bought by Peter Stuart, who became a wealthy man doing business with West Africa. He was also a homoeopath, offering his services for free. He was known as the Ditton doctor. After the Second World War, the house was divided into flats and demolished in 1959. We now see the houses in Southway that were built on the site.

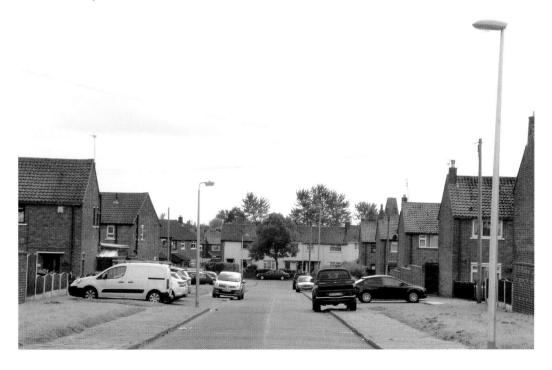

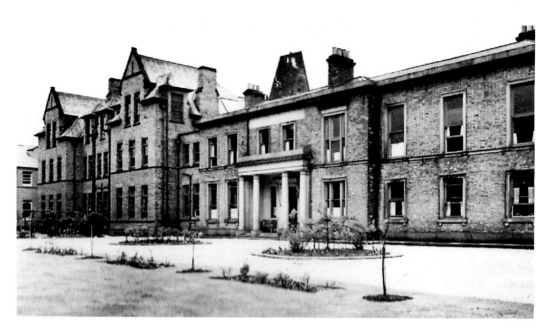

Ditton Hall (Nazareth House)

The house was built in 1829 by Bartholomew Bretherton for his daughter Sarah, who was a generous benefactor to the town. She established a school at the hall and later in 1860 built a separate school in Hale Road. She invited the Jesuits to live in the hall after her departure and provided money to build St Michael's Roman Catholic Church. The Jesuits left the hall in 1895 and the Order of Nazareth opened up a school for boys in 1903. The area is now occupied by desirable new homes.

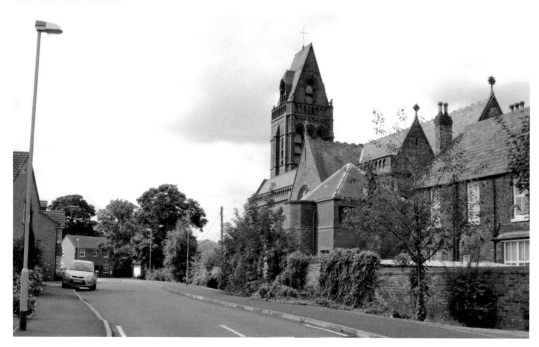

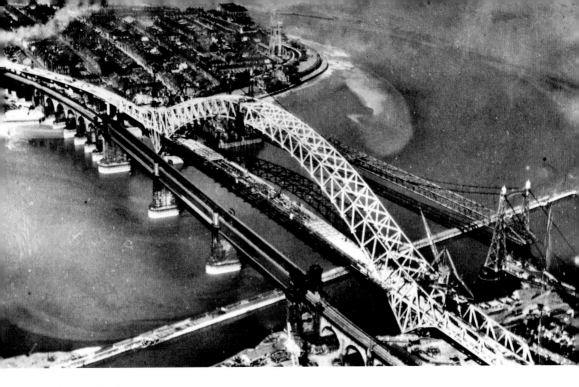

The Road Bridge

A view in 1961 of the new Widnes–Runcorn Bridge, which dominates the town. Opened in July 1961, it was widened in 1975 and renamed the Silver Jubilee Bridge in 1977 at the official opening ceremony. Sharp eyes will see that this high shot is taken from the Catalyst Museum on the Widnes side of the river.

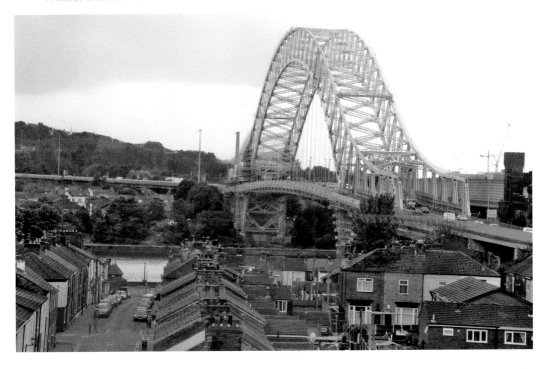

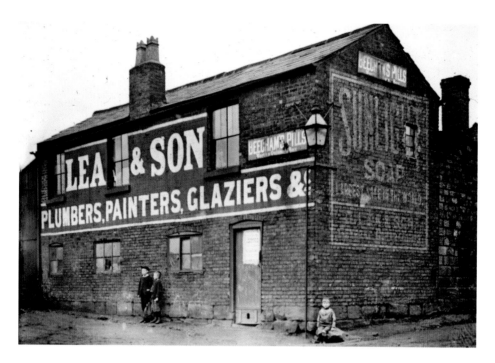

Old Farnworth Grammar Site

The site of the old Farnworth Grammar School at the top of Farnworth Street, built in 1580. We can still see a mark on the wall, which was where the headmaster's house stood. William Smyth Bishop of Lincoln endowed the school. Daniel Lea purchased the site of the old grammar school in 1860 for £30 and turned it into a successful painting and decorating business. Today, we see the corner with the church and the village shop.

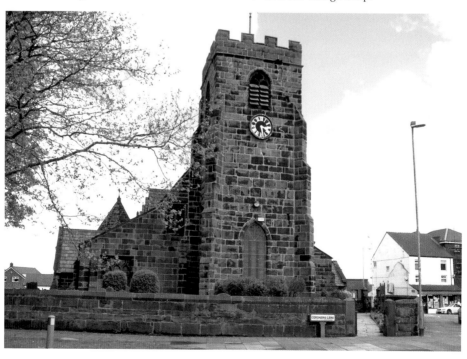

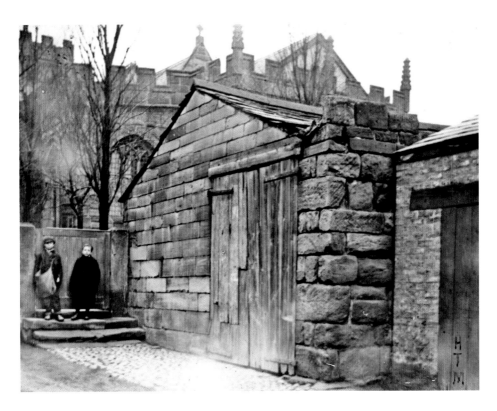

The Farnworth Bridewell

The Bridewell or lock-up of the village was built in 1827 to replace an earlier structure. Many a drunken man spent the night here. It fell into disrepair, but was restored in 2000 and now provides an interesting meeting place and a useful contribution to church life.

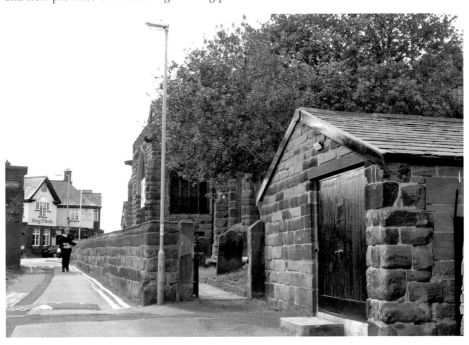

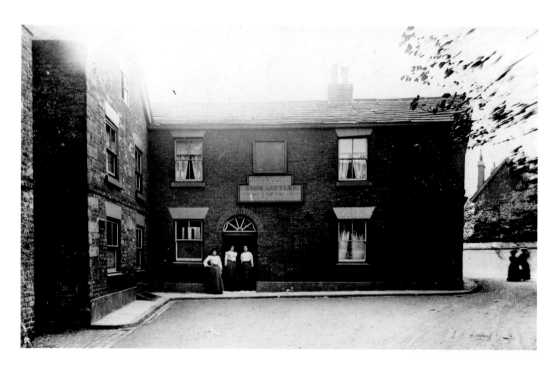

The Ring O' Bells

The pub has been much altered over the years. This picture shows the pub around 1890, when John Clare was the licensee and it was a farmhouse pub. He got into trouble for serving beer to non-travellers; it was only legal to serve people who lived over 3 miles away. Sadly, he enjoyed his own beer so much that he was often drunk and ended up bankrupt. The present building faces the church and has recently been refurbished and celebrated with a wonderful Jubilee party.

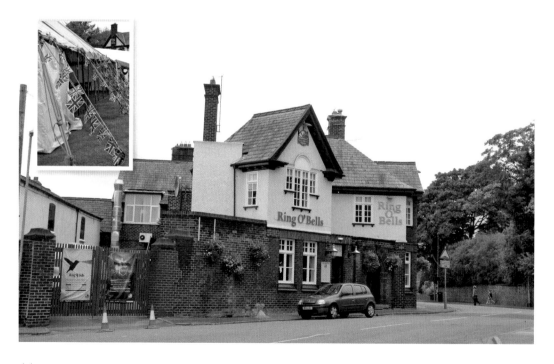

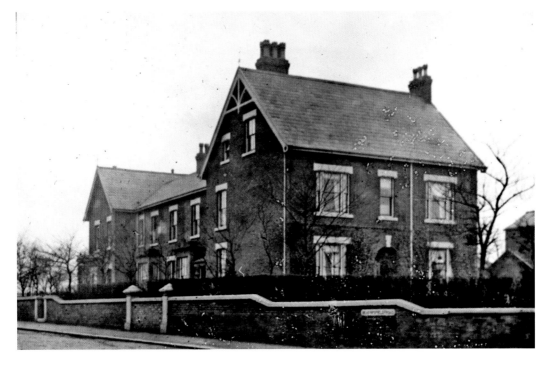

The Grammar School, Derby Road

This site on the corner of Derby Road and Beaconsfield Road was the Intermediate Grammar School. Mr James Raven was appointed headmaster in 1861, a fine teacher who paid for the required fittings from his own pocket. He was popular in the area, restoring the reputation of the school, and even building an extension to house boarders. It is now the home of Printel, a print and design company.

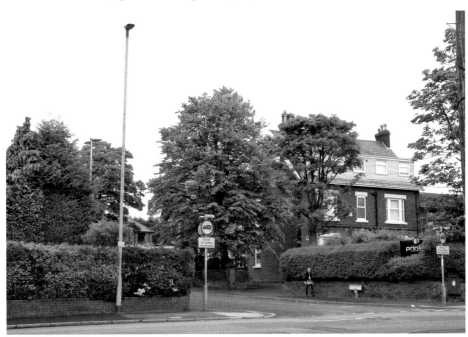

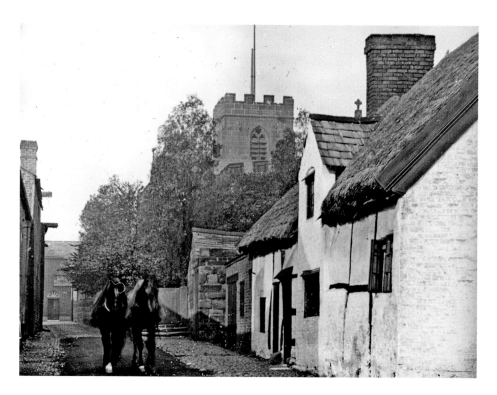

Marsh Hall Pad (School Brow)

This path was important to gain access to the church at the time of the plague, and was purchased by Bishop Smyth for his tenants from Cuerdley so that they could worship at the church without passing through Farnworth village. The old Sunday school is here and close-by is the site of the notorious bear-baiting, a feature of village life before the cruel sport was banned.

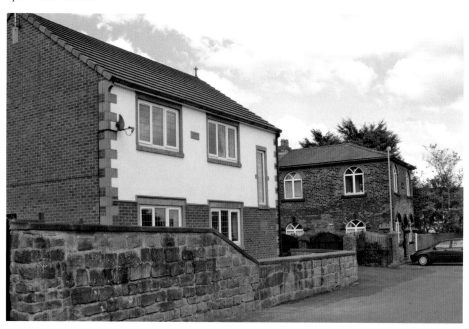

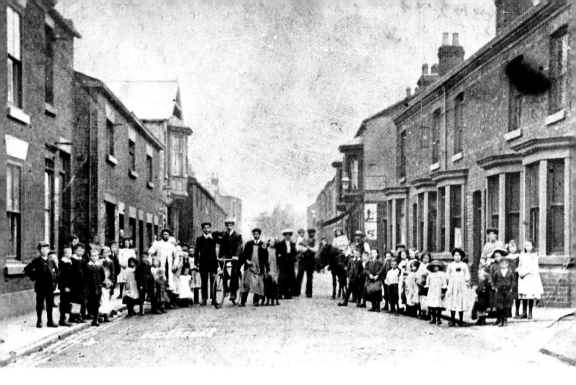

Church Street, Now Farnworth Street

Looking up the street around 1905. The tall building on the left, with the bay window, was Kirkham's bakery. Nearby was a busy sailcloth factory, a thriving industry of the time, as boat-building was an important local industry.

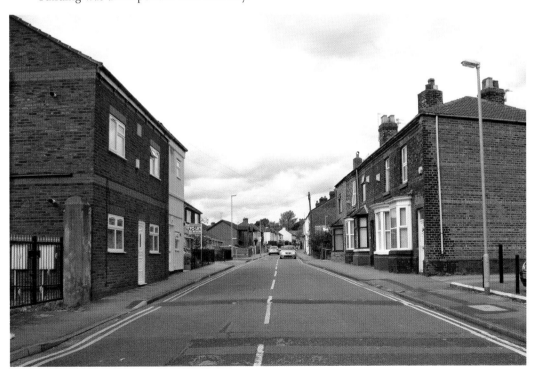

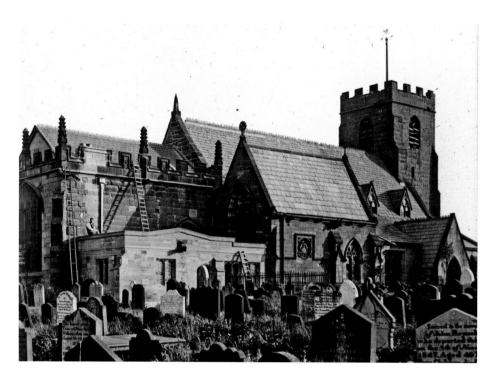

Farnworth Church

Farnworth was the principal village in the medieval period. The church was Saxon in origin and dedicated to the Saxon Saint Wilfred. It was developed by the Normans, who added the fourteenth-century tower. Originally a chapel of ease known as St Wilfred's in the parish of Prescot, it was rededicated St Luke's in 1859. This fine church is a fine memorial to the Bold family and their generosity to the people of Farnworth. Below, we see a wedding at the church and the edge of the SOS sign appealing to replace the church roof.

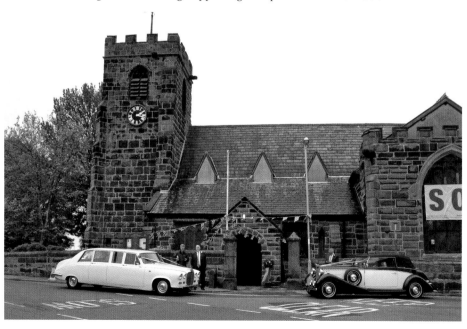

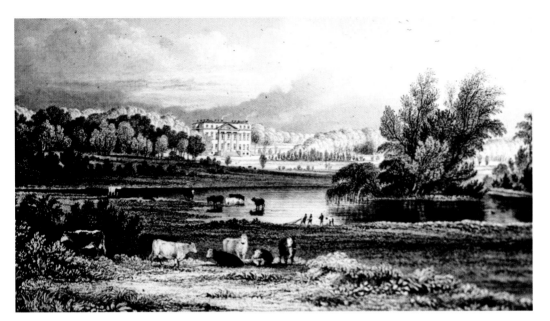

Bold Hall

A fine print of the new Bold Hall, built in 1732 by Peter Bold and designed by the Italian architect Leoni. Peter was the last of the line, which stretched back to Edward the Confessor. The original moated hall was built for the Bold family in 1616. The old hall outlasted the new one. To the right we see the tithe map of 1842, showing the extent of the estate and both halls.

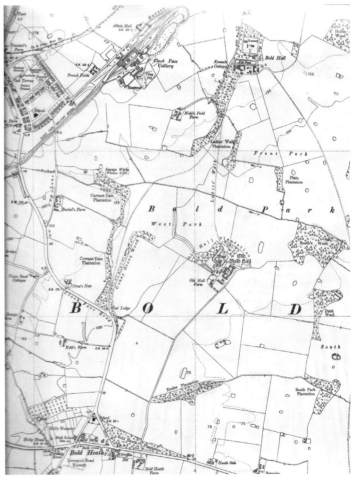

49

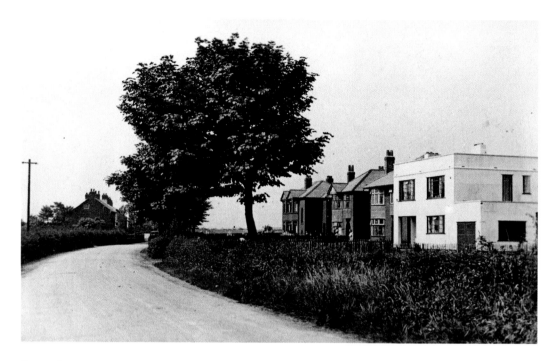

Upton Lane

Taken around 1936, this view shows the unusual Sunshine House, built in the thirties. At this time there was quite a fashion for these Mediterranean-style houses. Flat roofs and British weather do not really work. The house has been completely remodelled. On the right you may just be able to see the Upton Tavern.

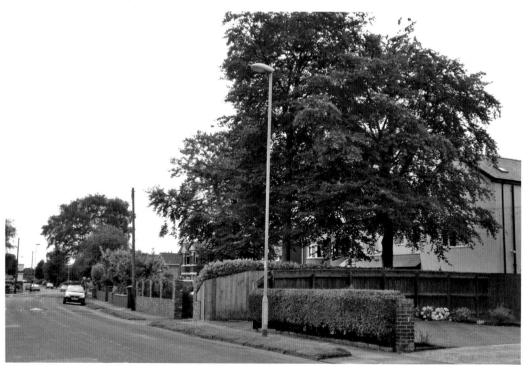

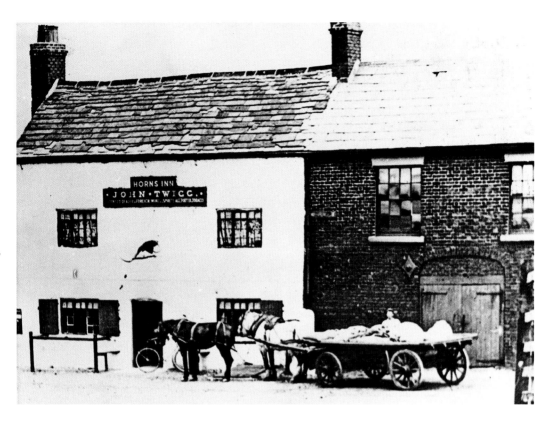

Horns Hotel

This old pub stood in Moorfield Road. It is believed to be named for the sound of the post-horn of the approaching coaches. This was, after all, the main road from Warrington to Liverpool. Today it is an industrial site and a busy roundabout.

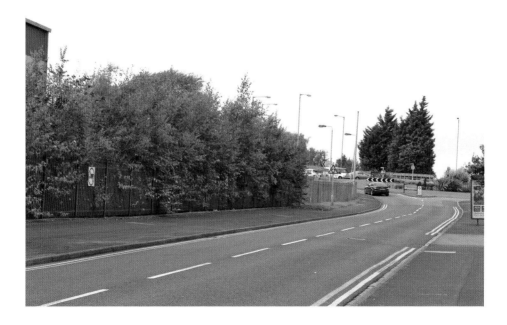

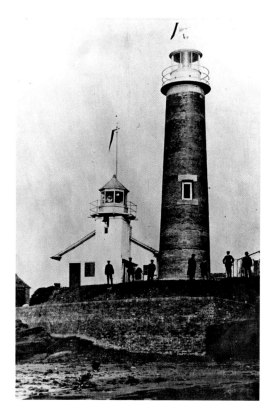

Hale Lighthouse

The Hale Lighthouse that you see standing today dates from 1906. Also shown is the shorter tower, built seventy years earlier around 1838. The tower is 45 feet high; the lamp's beam could be seen from as far away as 40 miles. The lighthouse was last used in 1958, when it was decommissioned. It still sits proudly on the sandstone cliffs.

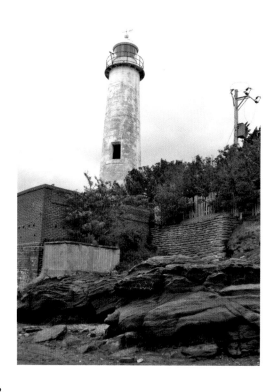

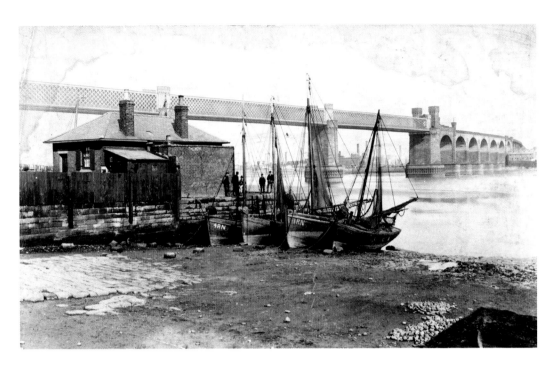

Railway Bridge from Runcorn Dock
A view of the railway bridge from 1890 showing the old ferry, fishing smacks and the ferry house beyond. No fishing boats now, but we can still see the remains of the dock.

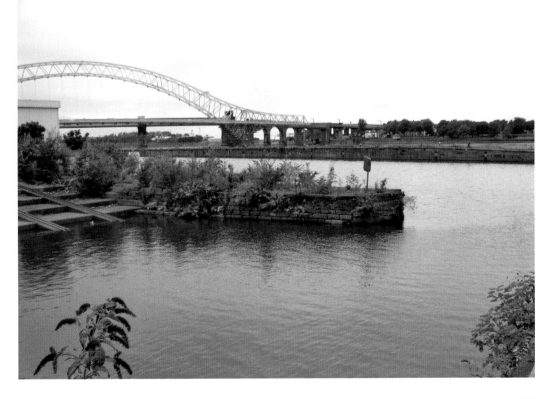

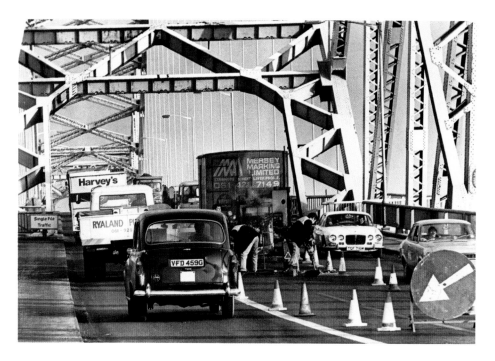

Road Bridge Traffic

Here we see the traffic on the bridge in 1970. The taxi driver is Tony Miller, driving a new Austin FX4. Nothing changes – roadworks are hindering the traffic, although in the current shot, surprisingly, the traffic is moving freely. The Mersey Gateway Project is a major scheme to build a new six-lane toll-bridge over the Mersey that will relieve the congested and ageing Silver Jubilee Bridge.

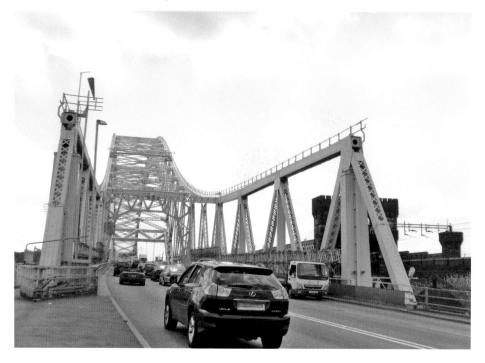

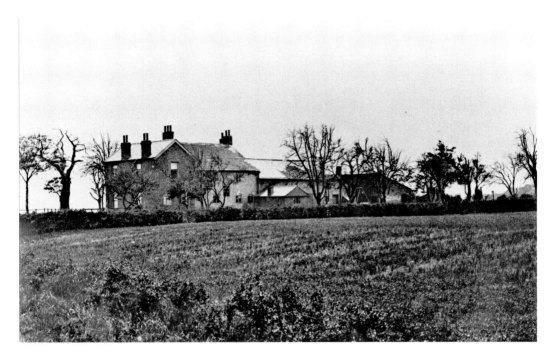

Mersey View, Halebank

Built around 1703, it has had several names. This was the home of John Thorburn, the owner of Ditton Iron Works. The works was the scene of a tragedy in 1876. An explosion killed six workers and a child who was bringing her father's breakfast. The legal documents name his home as Ditton Brook House. It was known as Mersey View for many years and is now called Shore House.

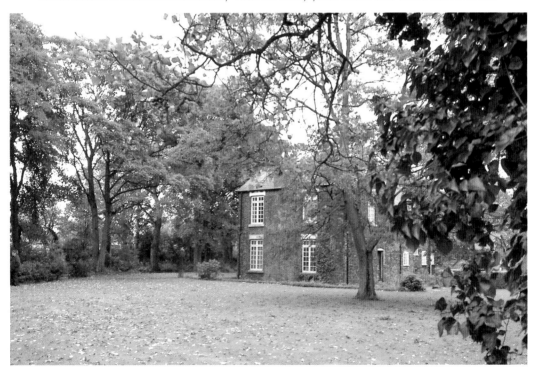

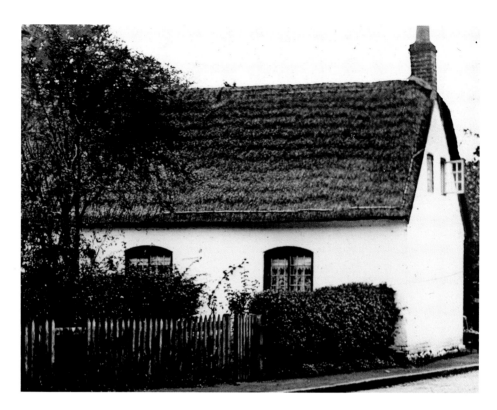

Childe of Hale Cottage

This was the famous man's home. He was a giant of the times and a local curiosity. Born in 1578, he was over 9 feet in height. In 1617 he was taken to London to meet King James I. The cottage is now being restored and was opened to the public for Heritage Weekend in September.

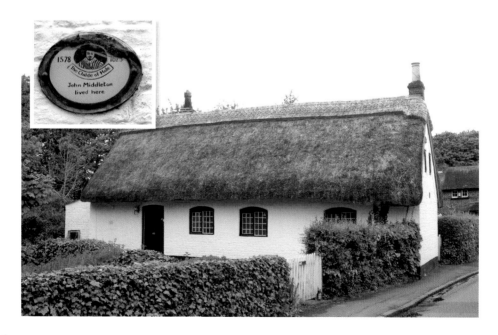

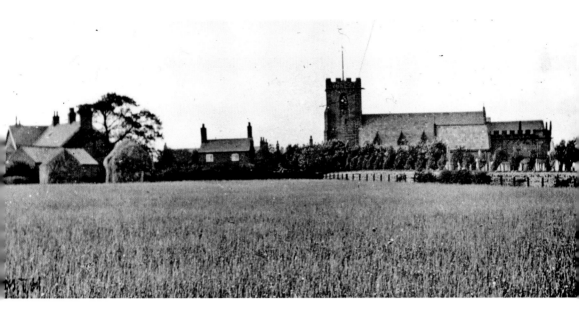

St Mary's Hale Parish Church

The chapel is of ancient origin, mentioned as early as 1260. The fourteenth-century tower is still standing, but the original black-and-white church was replaced in 1754, the benefactor being Colonel Ireland-Blackburn. Hale was in the chapelry of Childwall but was given separate status in 1828. The Childe of Hale is buried in the churchyard. The older view of the church is taken from the fields behind.

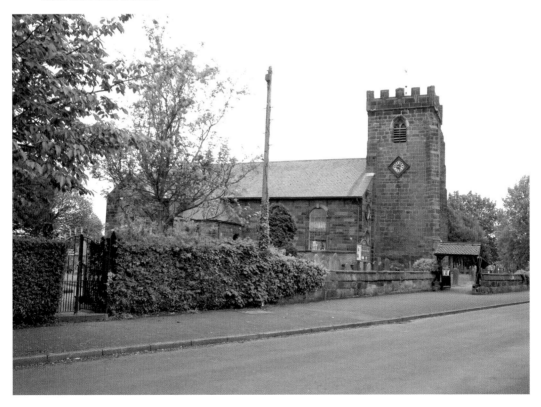

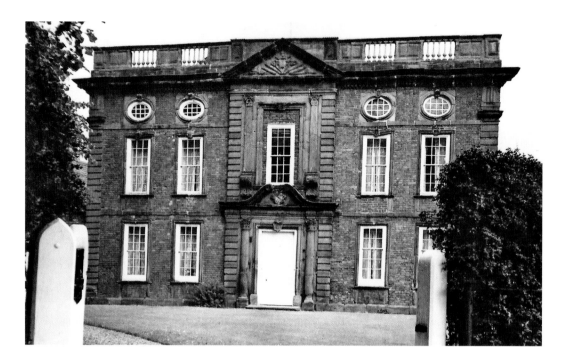

Hale Manor

When the Fleetwood-Hesketh family moved to Hale village in 1947, Hale Hall was beyond repair and so they took up residence in the old parsonage. It is now known as the Manor House. It overlooks one of the village greens and although the manor is much smaller than Hale Hall, the manor was even smaller in the past, as around the eighteenth century a west face was added by the Revd William Langford; his coat of arms and monogram are over the front entrance. It is still an elegant family home.

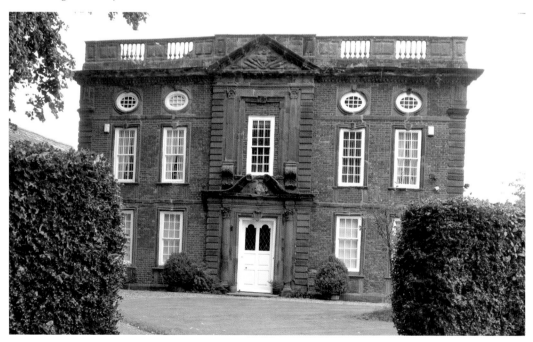

Wydnefs in ye olde Time.

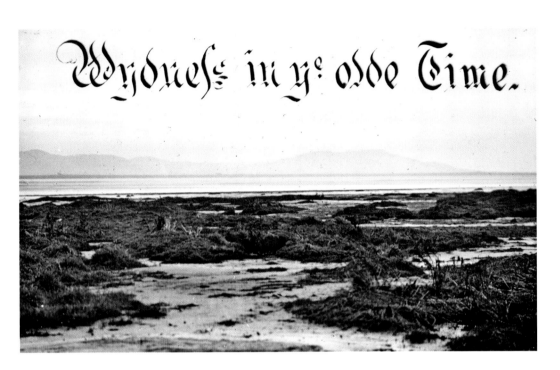

Widnes in Ye Olde Times
Who could have imagined how this view from Hale across the river would change. The Mersey Estuary is now dominated by the chemical works at Weston.

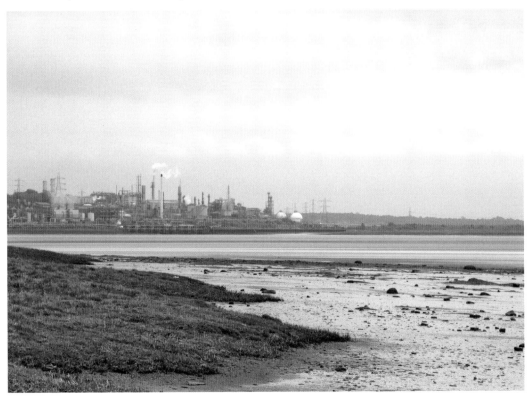

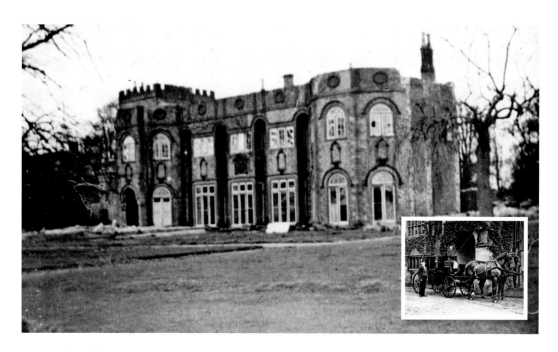

Hale Hall

The home of the Ireland-Blackburn family. The foundations were laid around 1620. In 1806 John Blackburn added a new south front to the hall, designed by John Nash. While the Ireland-Blackburn family lived at Hale Hall, many grand events took place. In 1932, a charity fête was held in the park and was attended by Sir Winston Churchill. Sadly, in later years the building became derelict, as this photograph shows, and was finally demolished. The only clue now to this grand house is the lodge house; we can see the family crest on the gatepost.

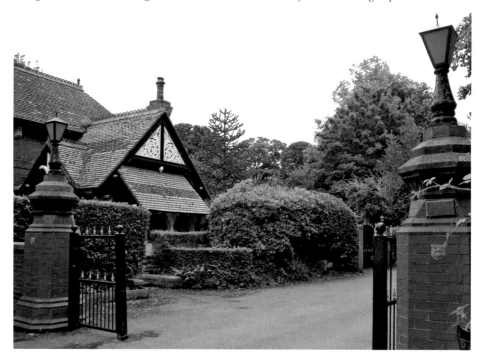

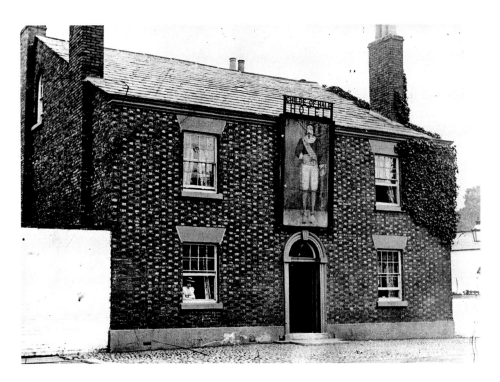

Childe Of Hale

The Childe of Hale was owned by Sir Gilbert Ireland, who also owned most of Hale village. A major feature was the portrait of the Childe of Hale. This was copied from a painting in Hale Hall by Thomas Berry. It was commissioned in 1889 and was the subject of a court case when the licensee refused to pay.

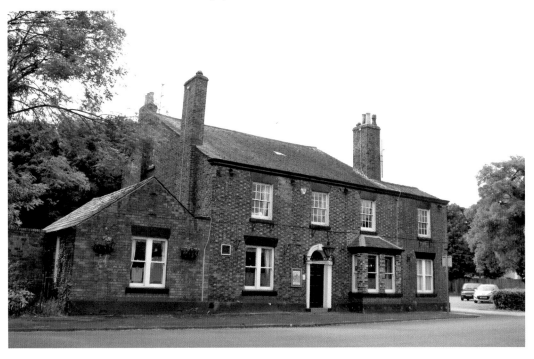

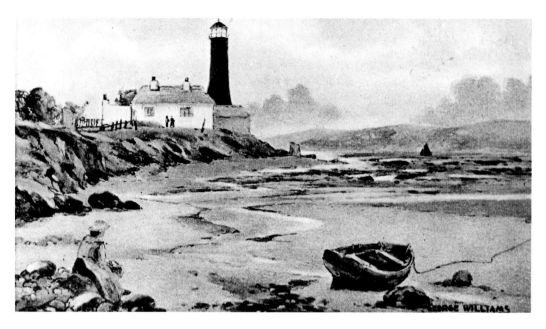

Hale Lighthouse
Another favourite view of the lighthouse from the shore. The path to the lighthouse makes a fine country walk and here we see the view in spring, the fields full of blossom.

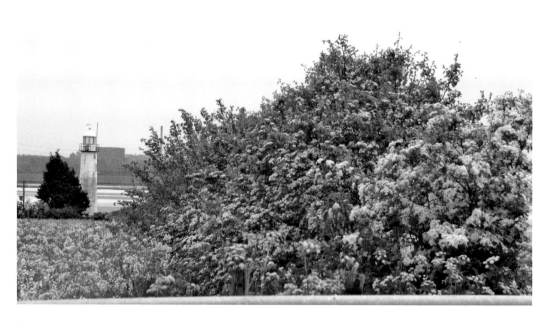

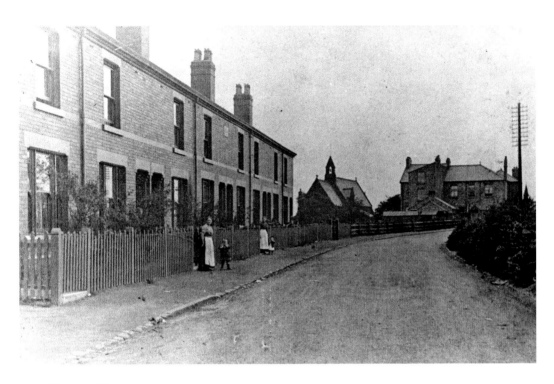

Liverpool Road

Taken around 1906, this view is of the terrace named The Laurels in Liverpool Road. St Michael's church can still be seen in this early view, but now shops have obscured the church.

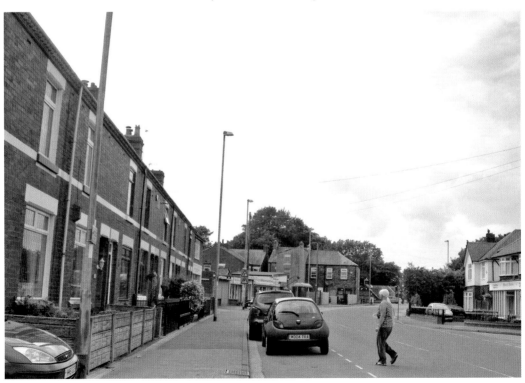

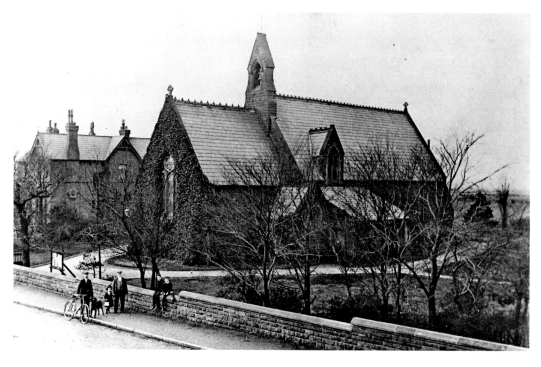

St Michael's, Church of England
A beautiful sandstone church, built in 1870. Thomas Shaw, the owner of Ditchfield Hall, provided the land. In 1877 the vicarage was added. These days the site is dominated by mature trees.

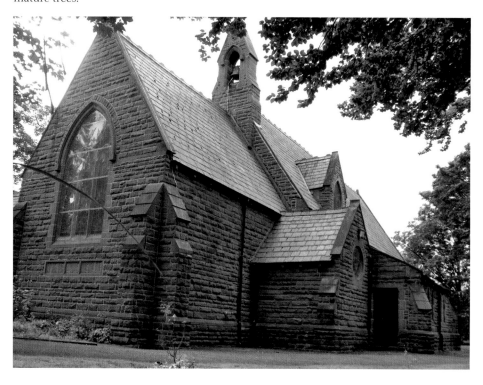

Ditchfield Hall

This fine building was originally moated, and was the home of the Dychfield family, devout Catholics who were persecuted for their faith. The Longton family rented the hall from the 1830s. A local butcher, William Stead, bought the hall in the 1920s and the last resident was John Laverick. The hall was treasured by locals and there were hopes to preserve it. Sadly, a fire in 1966 burnt the hall down and another fine building was lost to Widnes. The map of 1908 shows the position of the hall.

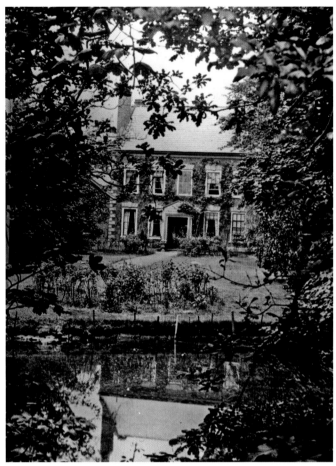

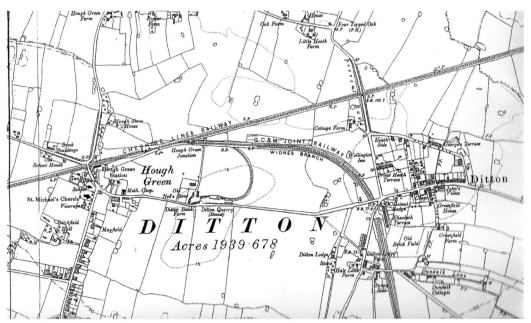

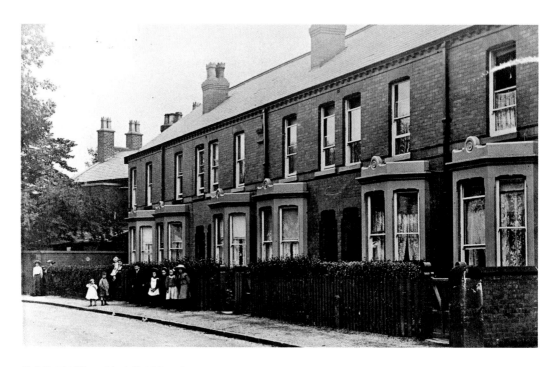

Oakfield Villas, Ditchfield Road

Everyone gathered here to watch the photographer in 1903. The detached house on the left was the home of Dr Robinson. Sadly it was demolished, but the fine row of villas still remains. We can see Oakfield on the 1908 map.

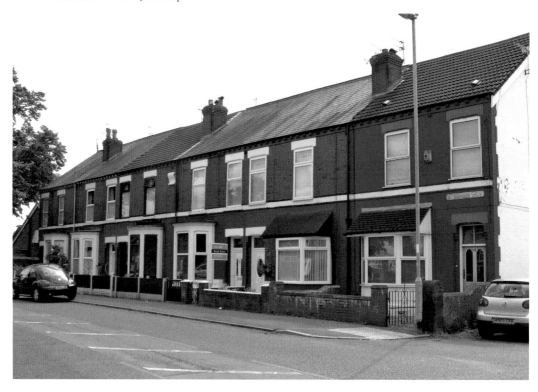

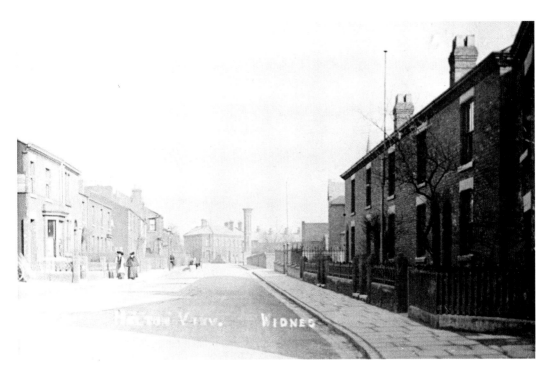

Halton View Towards the Castle Hotel

The Castle Hotel in 1908. It was on the site of an old farm called Woodcrofts. It replaced an old beerhouse. Perhaps the name derived from the view of Halton Castle across the river. We also see one of the old Victorian sewer-vent pipes. This is one of twelve vents that were situated around the town. Others were in Victoria Square and Simms Cross.

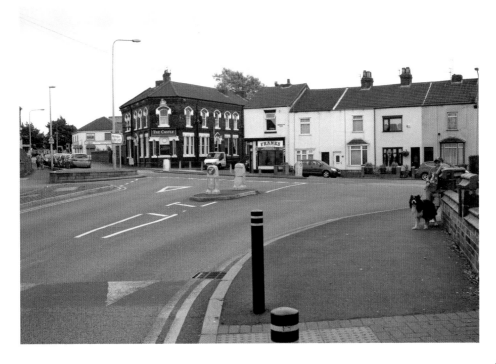

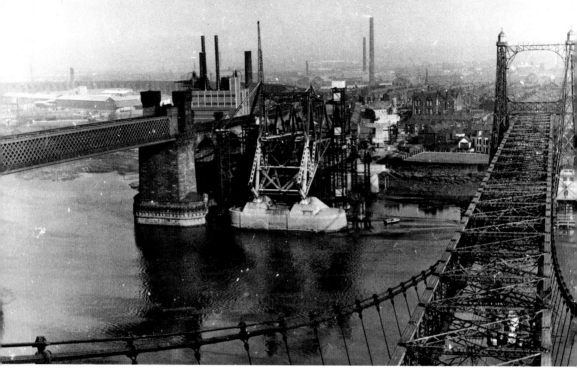

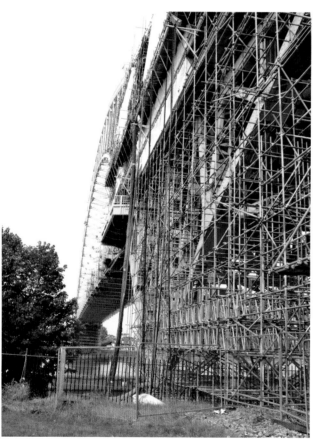

Widnes–Runcorn Bridge Construction
A view from the Transporter Bridge of the construction of the new road bridge around 1960. Continuous maintenance is essential; we see the scaffolding today during current work.

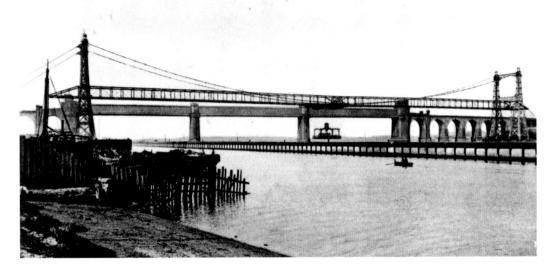

Two Bridges

We could not resist including this lovely photograph showing the two bridges before the road bridge. The equivalent photograph is taken from Runcorn, showing the railway and road bridge from the site of the new apartments in Mersey Road, Runcorn.

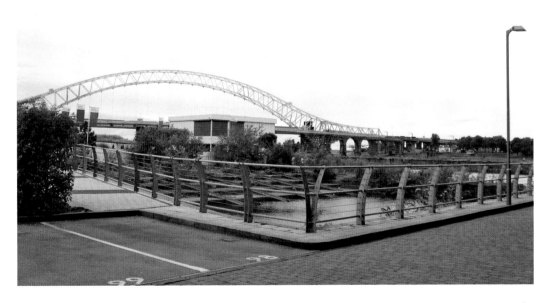

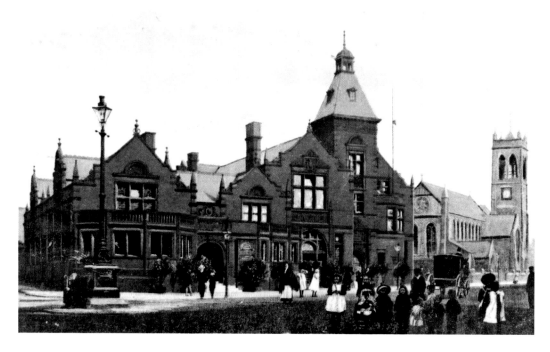

Widnes Library and Technical College

The Municipal Technical School and library were opened in 1896. Previously, the library had been housed behind the old town hall. Miss Procter, the librarian, decided to provide open access to the books. Children were not admitted, although boys were allowed to consult the newspapers. How very different now! Today it is a modern library with a café and excellent children's facilities.

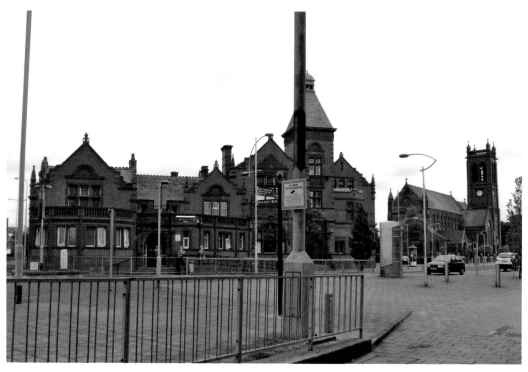

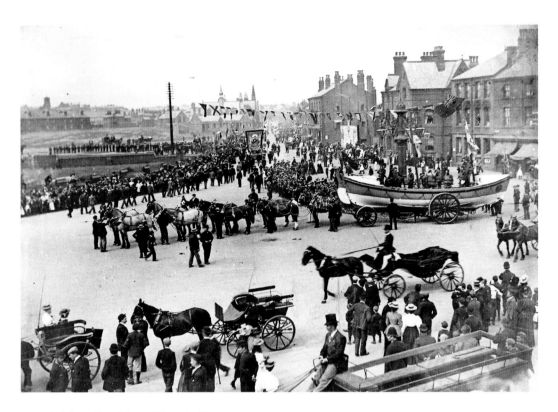

Widnes Road from Victoria Square

A fine scene in Victoria Square around 1890 celebrating Lifeboat Day. We are looking up Widnes Road towards Simms Cross. In the modern shot we can see the old post office and Broseley House.

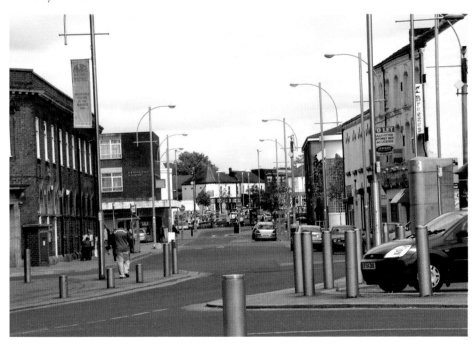

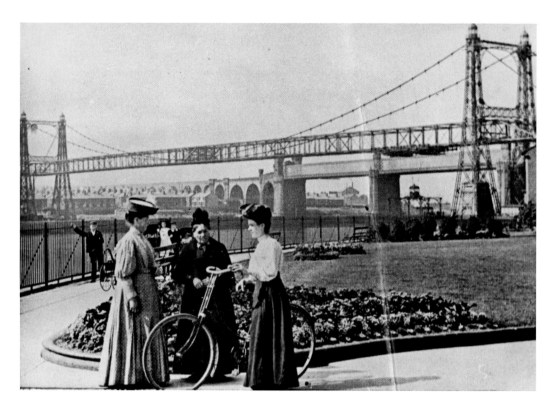

Victoria Gardens

In 1903, the original promenade was extended and a bandstand was built to commemorate Queen Victoria – a great place for relaxation. On Sunday evenings, a band would play. A fête was held every August. Families would go down to the beach to play games and enjoy sandcastle competitions. The ladies enjoying their cycling are dressed in their finest. No Lycra here. The Transporter Bridge is now long gone and the road bridge has taken its place.

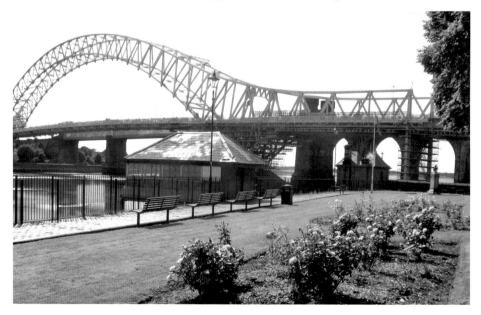

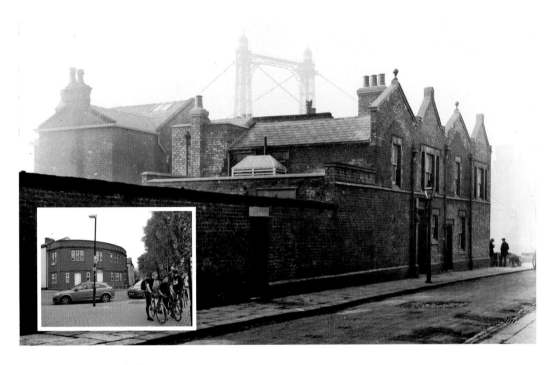

Accident Hospital

The industry of West Bank must have resulted in many serious accidents but it was not until 1878 that Widnes had its own accident hospital. The building looks imposing, but it provided excellent facilities. In its early days it provided only eight beds but was extended in 1914 to provide care for casualties of war. The hospital is now gone and just a red path shows the site. Bungalows have been built beyond.

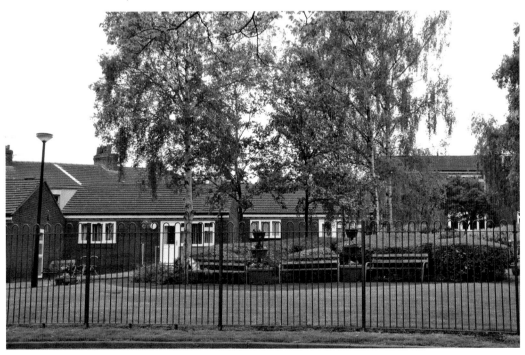

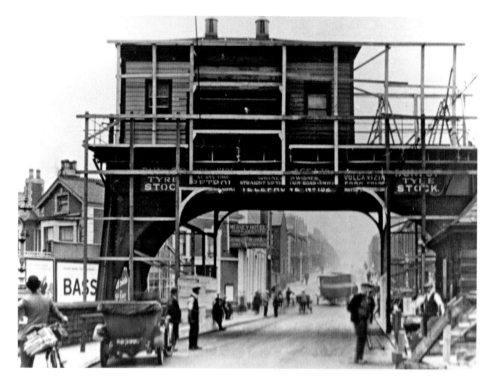

Mersey Road

A view up Mersey Road from the Transporter Bridge showing the Mersey Hotel. It was originally named the Boat House Inn as it was strategically placed for ferry travellers. In the 1930s the river was an important shrimping centre and it would have been full of shrimp boats. The pub is still known locally as 'The Snig', as shrimp pie (snig) was a delicacy of the house. When the new road bridge was opened in 1961, it bypassed Mersey Road and a once-busy street became much quieter.

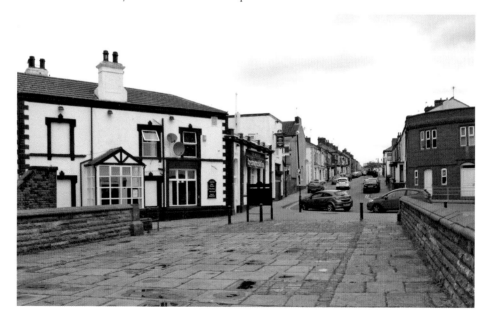

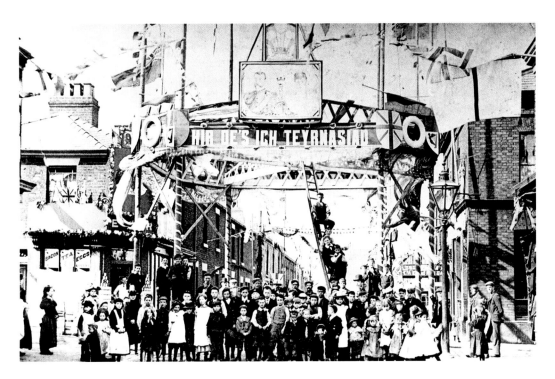

Welsh Arch

The Welsh arch was built to celebrate the Coronation of Edward VII in 1902 when West Bank was a thriving, busy community. This is the corner of Irwell Street. We see the strength of the Welsh community in West Bank; the sign reads 'Best Wishes To Your Reign'. The terraces still stand today but have been lovingly updated.

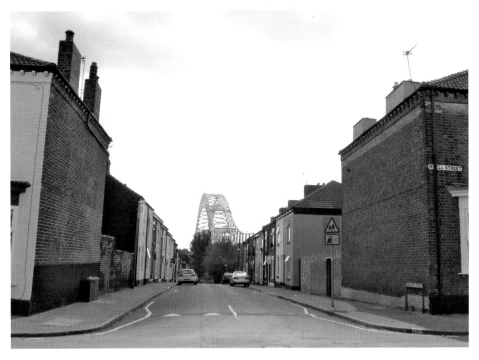

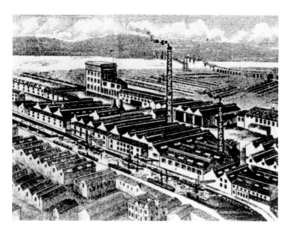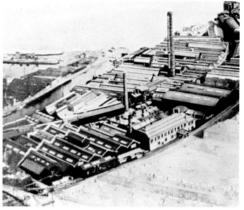

Gossage's Soap Works

In 1850, William Gossage opened his works. He started to produce his soap, quickly making the luxury product affordable to everyone. Here we see the amount of industry thriving in West Bank. Today we see green spaces and the magnificent Catalyst Museum, opened in 1989 by Viscount Leverhulme. The tower was built by Hutchinson but became the head office of Gossage's Soap Works. Catalyst is a unique museum dedicated to the chemical industry and a great place to visit for adults and children alike.

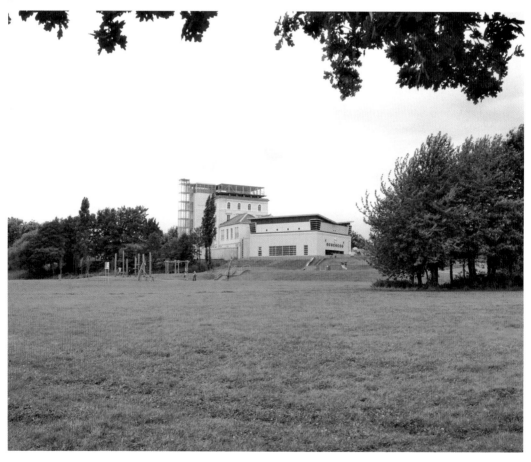

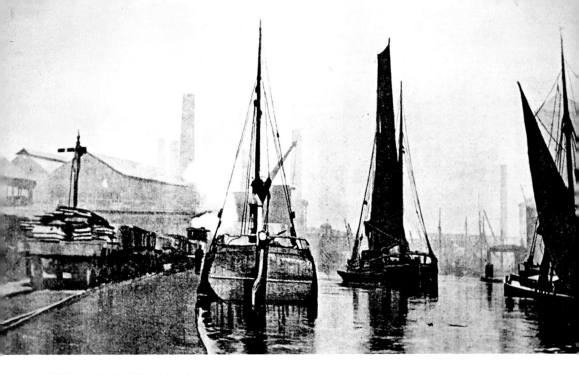

Widnes Dock, Spike Island

This was the birthplace of industry in Widnes. In 1847, John Hutchinson arrived from St Helen's aged twenty-two. He quickly saw the potential of this land and was able to purchase it for £12,000. The area was dominated by factories and a maze of railways crossed the island. In 1862, Ludwig Mond arrived in Widnes to inspect Hutchinson's work. John Brunner was the works manager. This was the start of the relationship which eventually became Imperial Chemical Industries. The land has been reclaimed and we now have an important haven for wildlife, and the waterside is enjoyed by boating enthusiasts and day trippers.

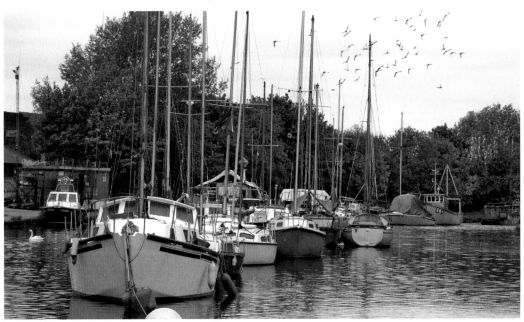

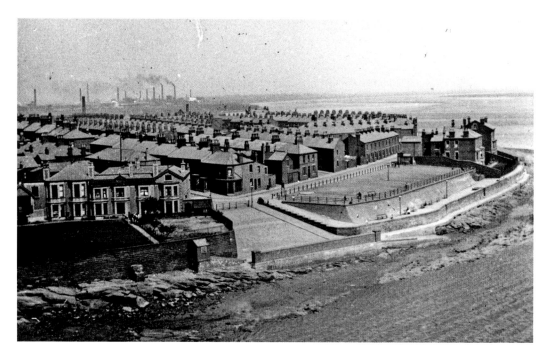

High View, West Bank

This photograph was taken from the railway bridge in 1896. We see West Bank prior to the building of the Transporter Bridge and the new St Mary's church. The promenade now has many mature trees and we can see Fiddlers Ferry in the background. Notice the red-brick building on the corner of Mersey Road, which was the Transporter Office.

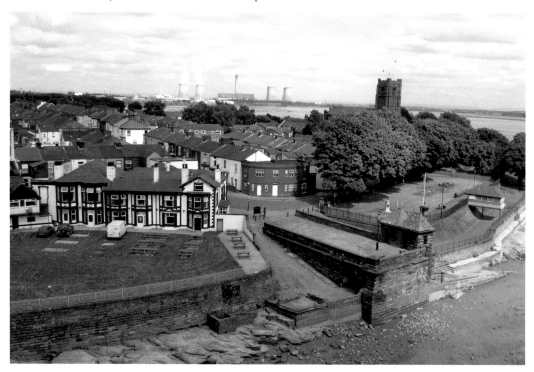

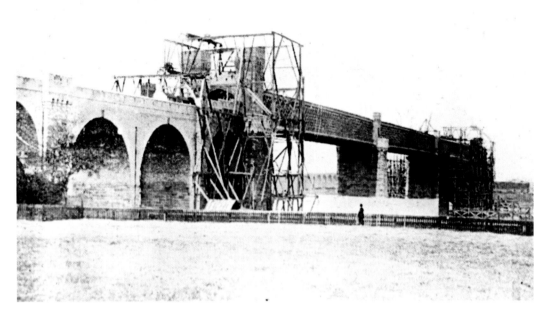

Railway Bridge

Crossing the Mersey has always been an essential part of life for Widnesians. The need to replace the old ferry was well recognised. The first plan was to build a railway bridge at Fiddlers Ferry but this came to nothing. Eventually the project was revised and the first stone for the bridge was laid in April 1864. This early glass negative shows the construction work. It was named Aethelfleda after the daughter of Alfred the Great, as the bridge was built on the site of her Saxon fortress.

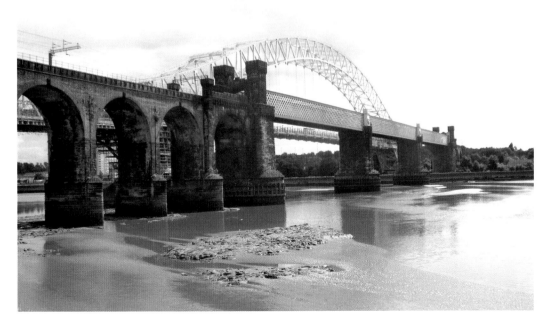

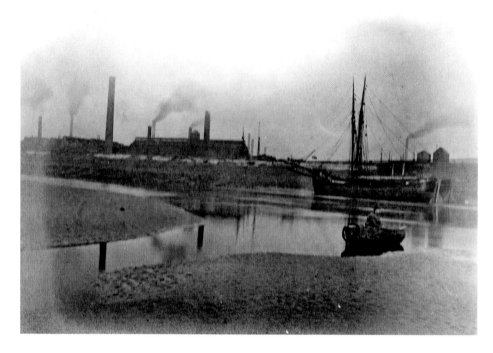

West Bank Dock
A view of the dock in 1890 showing Hall Bros and Shaw Works beyond. The dock was constructed by John Hutchinson in 1864. It was built to export his chemicals to the world, but by the late 1950s the trade had disappeared. Happily, it is now thriving again as the Mersey Multimodal Gateway and a Tesco distribution centre.

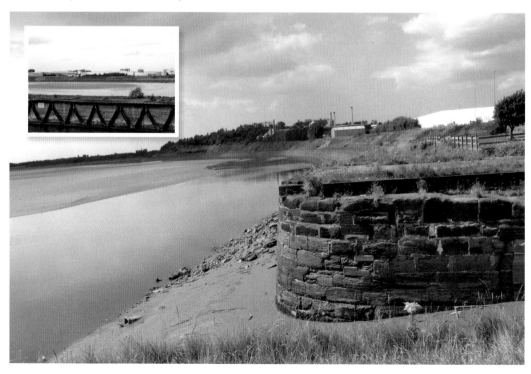

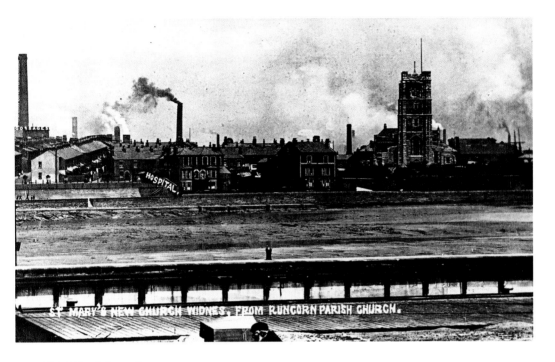

ST MARY'S NEW CHURCH WIDNES, FROM RUNCORN PARISH CHURCH.

West Bank from Runcorn

In 1910 we can see the new St Mary's church, the Accident Hospital and Gossage's factory. The Manchester Ship Canal is in the foreground. The smoking chimneys give a sense of the pollution of the time. Today the scene is quiet and the promenade is lined with trees.

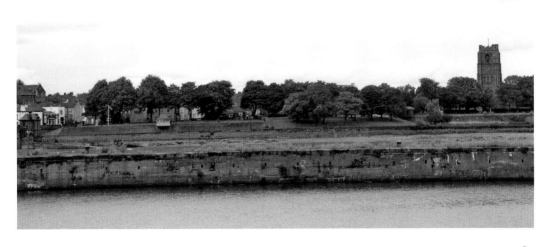

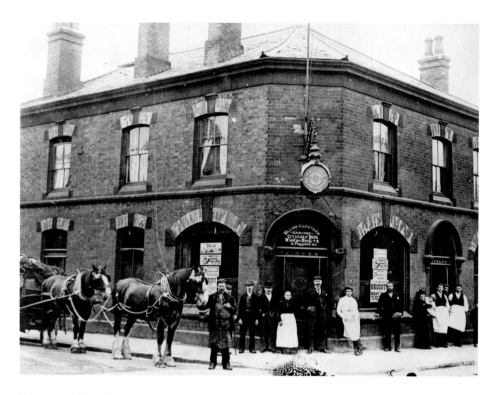

West Bank Hotel

Known as 'The Vaults' to West Bankers. Here the staff are proudly lined up outside this impressive hotel. It was built in 1864 by John Gerrard, but in 1938, despite its fine appearance, it was considered so dilapidated that it should be closed. Happily, it was reprieved and the building has now been transformed into flats.

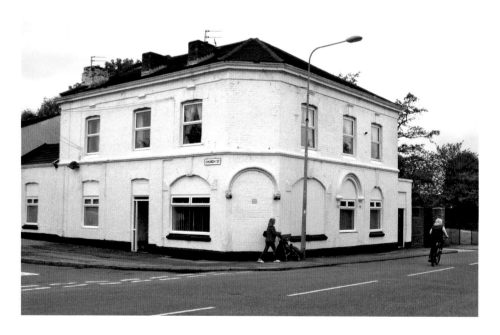

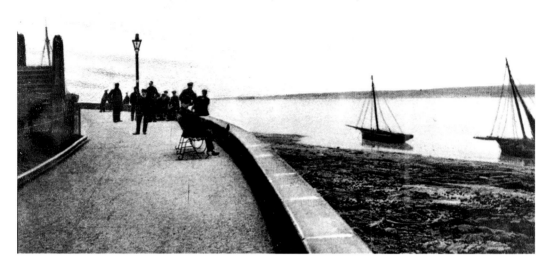

West Bank Promenade

In 1873, it was suggested that part of the flat, grassed area on the riverside should be turned into a promenade. Five years later work started and was completed in 1884. This scene at dusk with the boats on the river has a romantic quality. Today boats are a rare sight in the river, although the promenade is still enjoyed by West Bankers.

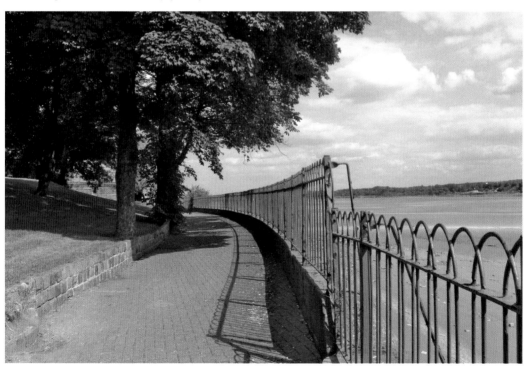

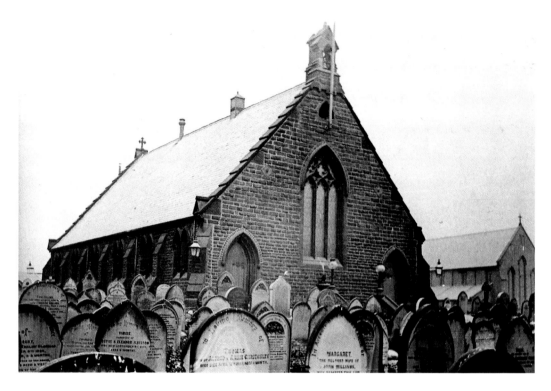

St Mary's Church

This is the first church, which was built in 1858 in Waterloo Road. It was built on chemical waste and by 1901 the walls were unstable. Over £11,000 was raised to build a new church overlooking the river. Mrs Gossage laid the foundation stone in 1908, her husband having donated generously to the new church fund. Here we now see the fine, red-stone church, built by Austin and Paley, standing proudly on the banks of the river.

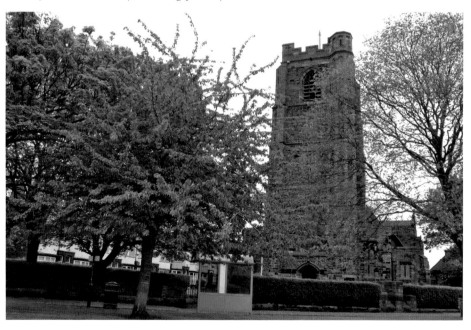

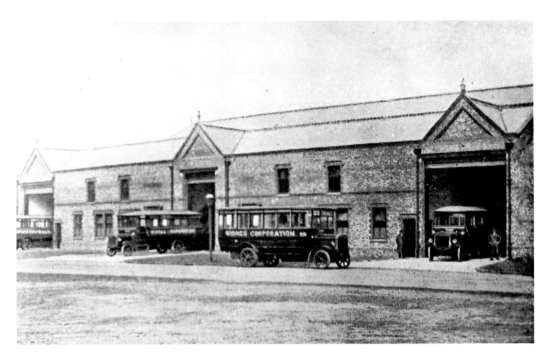

The Bus Garage, Moor Lane

A view of the new bus garage in Moor Lane taken in 1924. Moor Lane was a backwater at the time. Described as 'state of the art', a quotation in the newspaper stated, 'We're extremely proud of our elegant red-brick building with its fine terracotta detail.' Indeed it was a fine symbol of the town's pride. The building still stands today and the red brick has worn well.

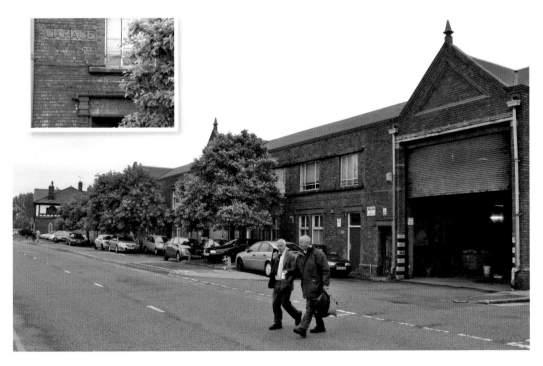

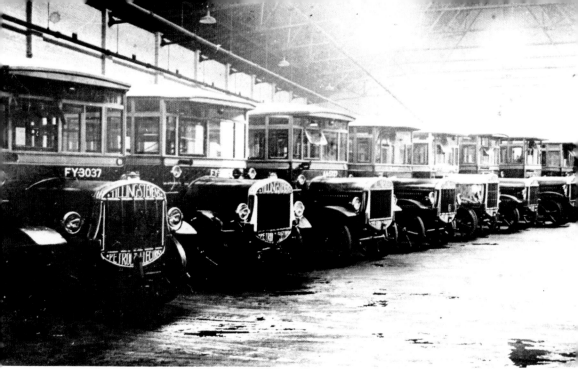

Bus Fleet

A fine display of Tilling Stevens buses lined up in the new garage. Today, unlike many areas, the bus company is still owned and run by the people of Halton. Here we see the fleet lined up behind the Municipal Buildings.

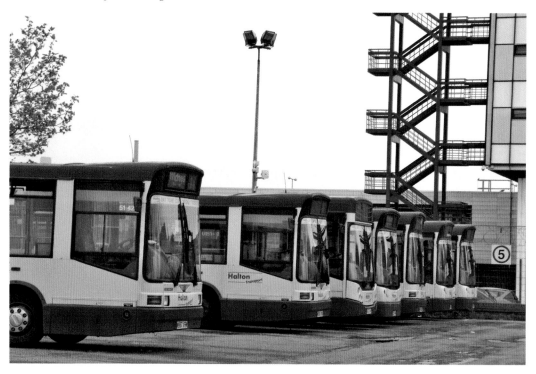

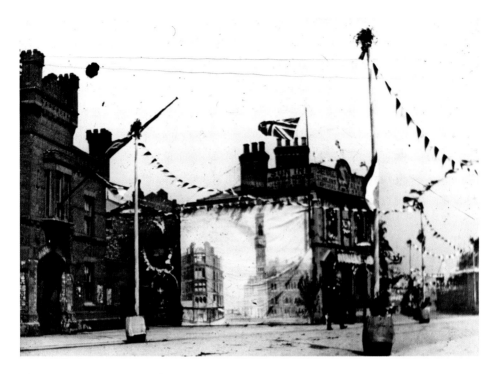

The Sun Inn, Victoria Road

The Sun Inn, proudly celebrating the Coronation of Edward VII in 1902. Either a mural has been painted or a drape has been put on the side of the inn. On the left can be seen the barracks of the 47th Lancashire Rifle Volunteers, which later became the Black Cat Billiard Hall. The pub is now named Kelly's and we can see the flags for Queen Elizabeth's Diamond Jubilee. The name change was a reference to Ned Kelly, as an Australian took over the licence.

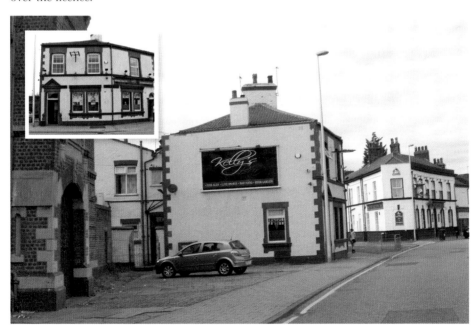

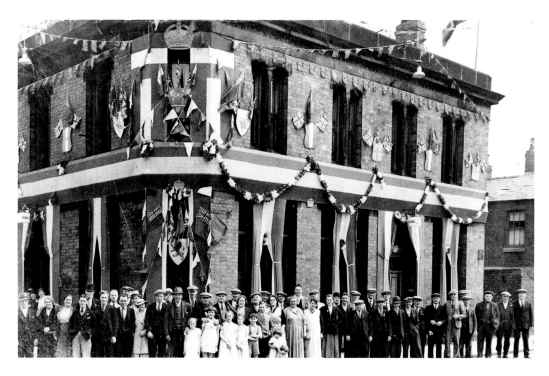

Prince Of Wales, Kent Street

The Prince of Wales public house in Kent Street, decorated to celebrate the Silver Jubilee of King George V in 1935. The pub was commonly known as Reidy's after the publican, Billy Reid, who was an ex-Widnes rugby player. The pub is now looking rather forlorn and despite its position by the busy shopping centre it is now sadly closed.

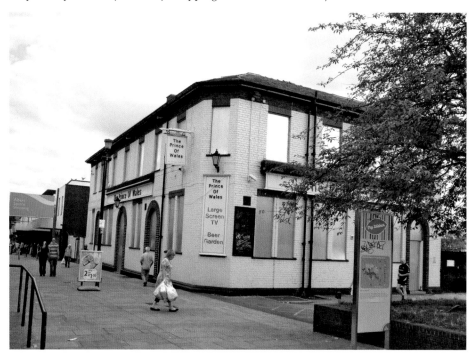

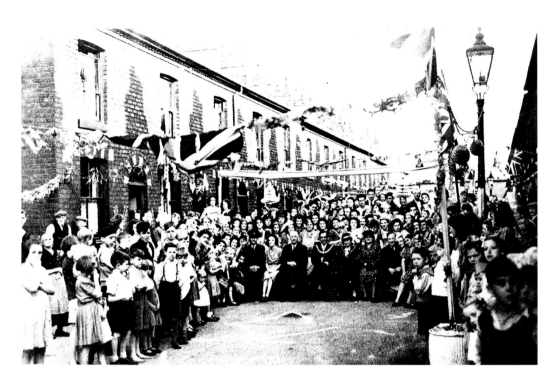

Marrabone

Celebrations for VJ Day 1945 in Marrabone, the area around Bedford Street, Walmsley Street and part of Warrington Road. We can see Mayor Richard Yates and Mayoress Mrs Yates. The photograph shows the community spirit that we have now lost. The houses are demolished, and we now have these rather sad industrial areas.

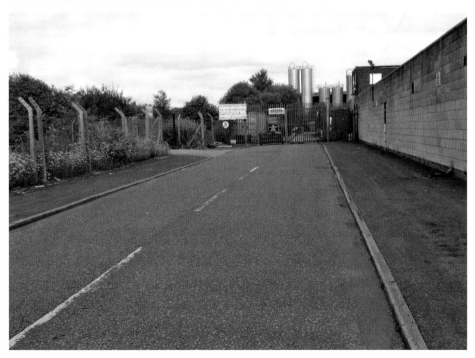

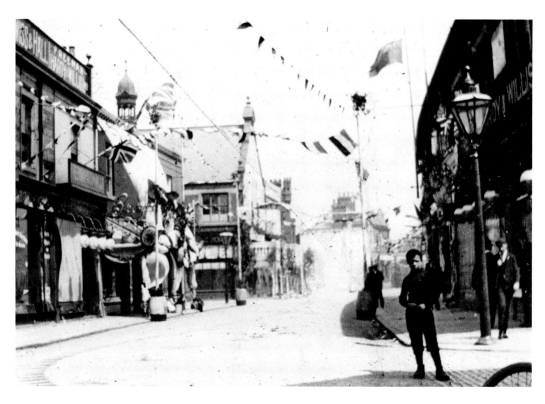

Victoria Road

Another shot of Victoria Road in 1902 with the Sun Inn in the background. This is a rare glass negative, which accounts for the quality of the photograph. The boy in the foreground is taking a great interest in the photographer. The road is now transformed.

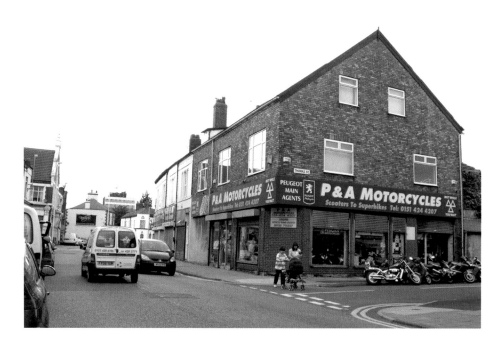

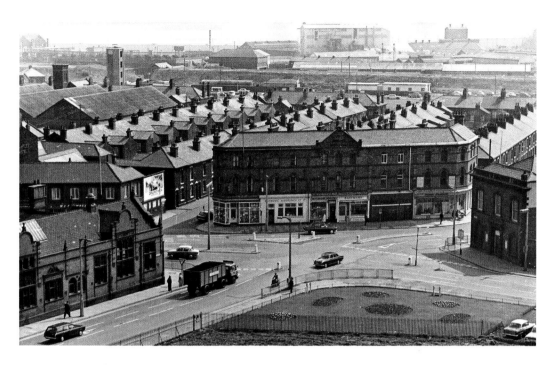

Kingsway from Municipal Buildings

This is taken from the top of the Municipal Buildings before the new roundabout was built. Showing shops, the library and old police station on the corner of Victoria Road. Kingsway was named St Bede's Way until 1913 when George V visited the town. They drove up the newly named road to visit Victoria Park and then departed by royal train from Farnworth Station. Now we see the new Job Centre and Health Centre.

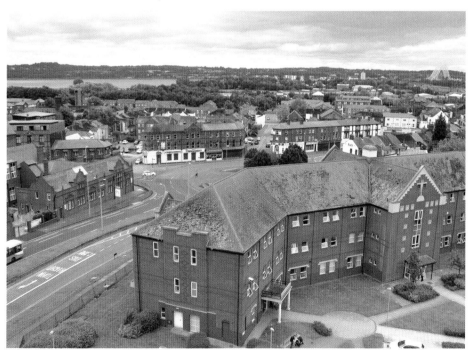

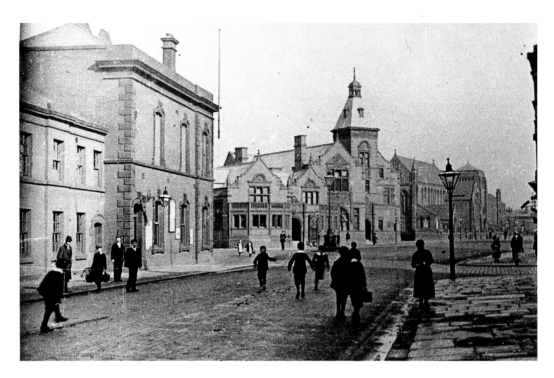

Victoria Square from Victoria Road

A delightful picture of Victoria Square around 1900. Taken from Victoria Road, it shows the police station on the left, which is now Rui's – a music bar. We can see St Paul's church before the spire was added.

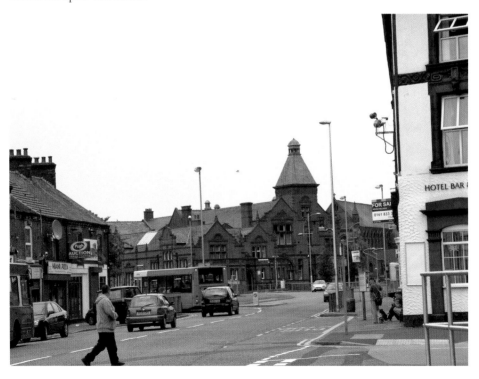

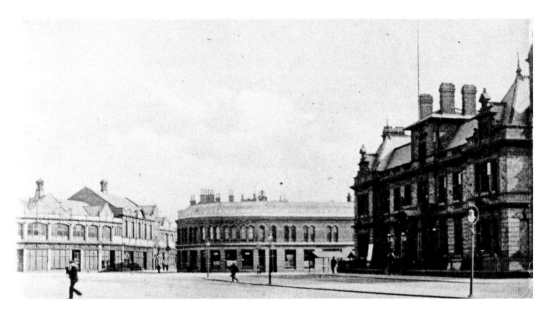

Victoria Square

This view of the square shows the Co-operative store and the Market Hotel around 1910. The hotel was built to serve the new market hall and the Victorian architecture really enhanced the square. The fine old town hall is now a nightclub, The Establishment. Today we still see an impressive square.

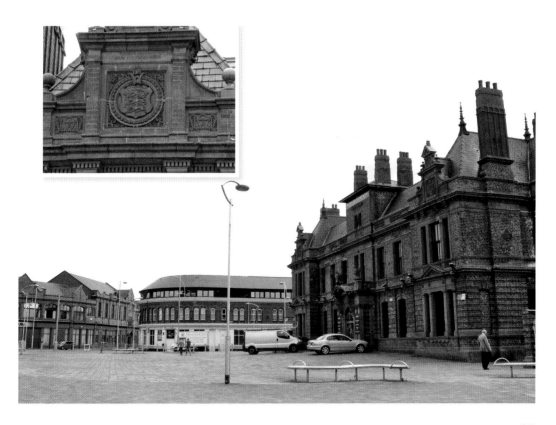

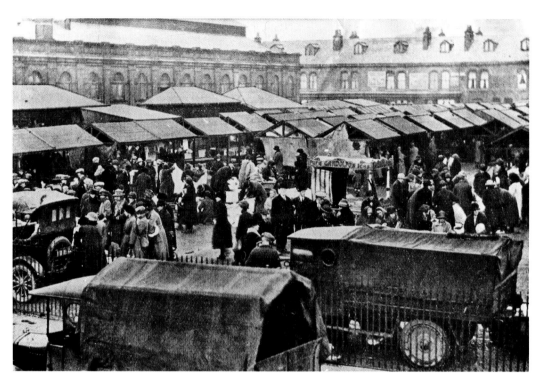

Widnes Market

In 1875 a market hall was built in Victoria Square, and what a bustling scene we see. Widnes market is still prospering but it has now moved to the Green Oaks area of the town.

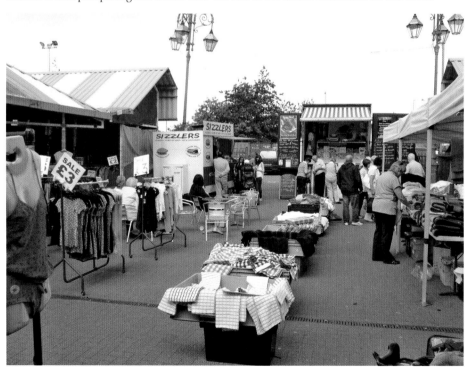

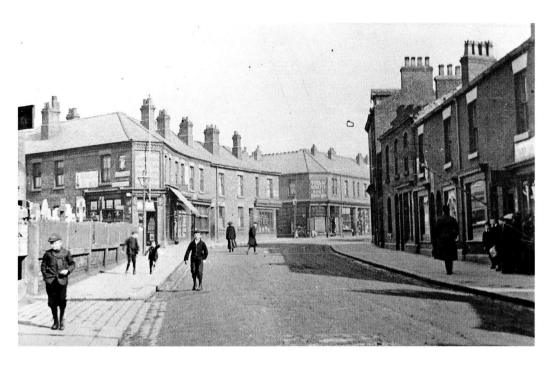

Widnes Road, Simms Cross

What a change: from a road full of local shops and no cars to the view today. The Old Simms Cross School was here. The primary school is now in Charles Street. The area is now dominated by the ASDA store and its large car park.

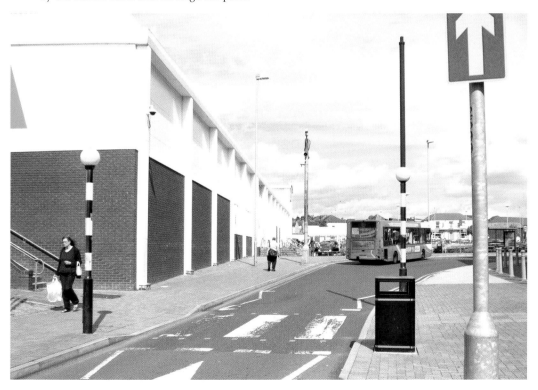

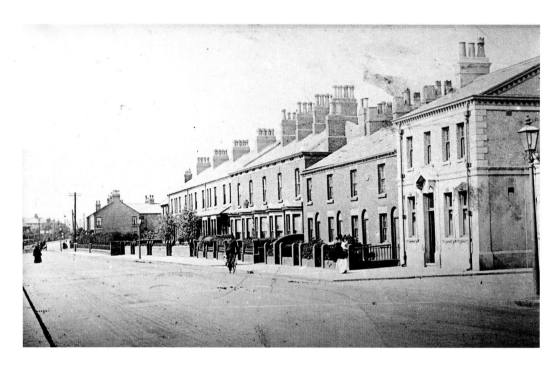

Birchfield Road

The Horse & Jockey stands alone on the modern picture. It was once part of the terrace. Originally, a beerhouse named The Greyhound stood on the site. Happily, the fine terrace with its bay windows still stands today.

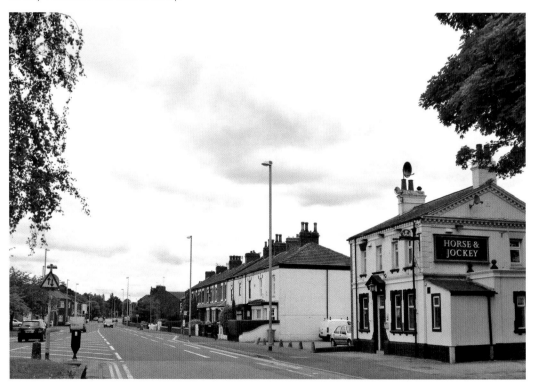